Professional Walk

An Educator's Perspective

by

Rechel M. Anderson, Ed.D.

Professional Walk

Copyright © 2022 by Rechel M. Anderson

All rights reserved. No part of this book may be reproduced, scanned, or distributed in any printed or electronic form or by any means without prior written consent of the publisher, except for brief quotes used in reviews.

Published by
Hadassah's Crown Publishing, LLC
634 NE Main St #1263
Simpsonville, SC 29681

ISBN: 978-1-950894-97-0
Library of Congress Control Number: 2022922720

Printed in the United States

Professional Walk

To Marlene Sims, Children (Antonio, Brittany, and Erin), Parents (Richard & Mozella), Brother Richard, my late loving Grandmother Mozella, and my mentor, Calvin Wallace

Professional Walk

Foreword

Every teacher, coach, or mentor delights in seeing his/her student or protege thrive. Such is my sentiment and pride over Dr. Anderson academic and published accomplishments. This written work is a testament to your strength, perseverance, and courage as a leader. Rechel, you have gone through the refinery of life, and have come out on the other side triumphantly. Dr. Anderson has a story to tell. My sincere hope is that the words found in this book will fall on fertile ground through each reader and sprout, grow, and help replenish the educational draught that is prevalent in many school districts across this country, especially during this pandemic.

May God bless you and keep you in his care.

My Love to You,

Kathi

Kathi Gibson, PhD

Professional Walk

Professional Walk

Contents

The Foundation	5
The Belief	27
The Promotion	48
The Principalship	68
The Superintendency	109
Acknowledgments	133

Professional Walk

CHAPTER ONE

The Foundation

Small southern towns are a special type of magic. In my experience, that magic was made up of gospel songs, long drives, and Grandma's house. My small town was probably no different than any other, but it was mine and I loved it. Growing up in Florence, South Carolina taught me much about myself and life. It was on church pews that I learned the value of faith, around our kitchen table where I learned about the importance of family, and in my community where I learned respect. It was also there, in that small town, far from big cities, that I became me. My foundation is so tied to that place, to those memories, and those lessons. When I look at my life now, I can't help but find the bedrock of my experiences in that small town.

My world was made up of my family: my dad, my mom, my brother, and my grandma Mozella. My grandmother didn't live far from us in town, so I always felt like I had two homes. If I wasn't at my house, I was sure to be at Grandma's. Being at her house was especially nice because my brother and I could walk to Mr. Grady's corner store or Stokes Gas Station and get a big bag of our favorite ten cent candies.

With a handful of *Now and Laters* and *Red-Hot Fire Balls*, my brother and I would hang out at Grandma Mozella's while she was usually doing something for church. Although we were expected to be on our best behavior and mostly seen and not heard, Grandma Mozella often hosted church folks at her house for gatherings. It wasn't odd to see the pastor stop by regularly to check in. In our small town, with our strict parents, most of our social outlets came from church. Hanging out at Grandma's house was something to do and it was always nice when, on the off chance, someone from church brought their children or other young people we could spend time with.

It was always important to Grandma that we see what it meant to live a God-fearing life; in fact, it was a core tenant of our family. My parents would always say that our foundation was God, family, and respect. Sundays were a big day in our family because of that. Saturday nights were filled with planning for Sunday mornings--picking the best clothes, making sure they were ironed and crisp; taking my nightly shower and ensuring that my hairstyles would be in perfect condition in the morning. I always had to make sure that my Bible was by the door the night before so there was no excuse to be late. I remember Sunday mornings started with gospel music on the radio filling the house while everyone individually got up and ready on our own. My brother and I knew that brushed teeth and washed faces were first in order before we went to the kitchen to help with breakfast and morning chores.

Both of my parents attended church, but my mother grew up Southern Baptist and my father grew up in the Pentecostal Holiness church. Although both religions knew how to praise God, my brother and I secretly got up just a little bit earlier to make sure we were going to church with my mom. If you're familiar with Pentecostal Holiness church services, you know that they can go on and on, which meant you were bound to be hungry and tired by the end of it, and a little bored during it. Thankfully my dad didn't care where we went to church as long as we went. He would always say that God only asks one day of us, and we should look forward to starting our week with the word of God.

Church was a central part of our lives and a strong social outlet as well. Over time I embraced my relationship with God, but like any other child, church started out as a requirement.

Attending church was a way for me to see other kids my age and have a little fun, since weekdays were for school and extracurriculars, not hanging out. My family was very involved, so we went to church conferences, Vacation Bible School, youth choir practices, and beyond Sundays, we were sure to be at mid-week services on Wednesday. As my brother and I grew older, my grandmother would start asking us about what we learned from the sermons and how we planned to incorporate the teachings into our lives. It was that foundation that let us know that church was to be taken seriously and would eventually teach me how to cleave to those teachings when life became challenging.

Sundays were undoubtedly for church, but they quickly became my favorite day of the week because those were our ice cream days. Our family had a tradition of long drives to the ice cream show, and then we'd go to the park afterwards. Once we finished with services, my brother and I would hop in the back of my dad's big, bodied Buick and wait for the engine to turn over. My mother sat in the front seat, with my dad driving, and we'd head down the road with visions of butter pecan and strawberry double scoops. I loved everything about those rides. I loved the Buick we rode in. It was big and loud and made us feel like we were in the movies. You know, those movies where life seemed effortless, and you could just 'be.' Maybe it was because we were young, or maybe cars are just built differently now, but that car felt so large and spacious. We could stretch our legs and feel the wind on our faces as we barreled down the street.

Our mouths watered thinking about our favorite ice cream orders, but it turns out that the ice cream wasn't the highlight of those trips. We laughed and joked around with each other, sang along with the radio, but most notably, we'd just be ourselves with each other. We talked about our lives and what was important to us. Sometimes that was school, other times that was our dreams, and other times it was just about what was going on in the world around us. Those rides always made me feel so close to my family, and I have to thank my dad most for that.

My dad's name is Richard, just like my brother's -even though he's not a senior- and he is one of my favorite people. My dad is a retired Army veteran and though he was the disciplinarian of the family, he has always been a gentle and loving father. He was stern and regarded himself as the protector and provider for our family. My dad was a great communicator, but he also knew how to tell you he was serious with his eyes as well. It only took one look from him to know that you needed to straighten up and remember what he'd taught you. I have always admired my dad's ability to balance great discipline yet offer gentleness within himself. He managed to provide me with a strong foundation of core values while also allowing me the space to be myself.

I remember on one particular Sunday I was at my grandma's house sitting on her front porch. A neighborhood boy was riding his bike and stopped at her gate and started talking to me. I knew him from church and while I didn't think much of him before, I could tell by the way he was talking that he had a crush on me. He was being playful and asking a lot of questions, so it was clear that he liked me. I was in eighth grade at the time, so I didn't fully understand the boy-girl relationship thing. Naturally, I was a bit mesmerized by him. It felt nice to have him like me. After talking for a bit, we planned to meet after Sunday school that coming week.

When we were at my grandma's house we weren't allowed to go beyond the gate or allow anyone in, so this conversation all happened where my grandma could hear me. I thought she was in another part of the house but as I walked back inside, it was clear that she had heard everything. She immediately let me know this and promptly reminded me of our family's expectations around dating. As a young lady, it wasn't proper for me to plan to see a boy. He was supposed to meet my family so they could get to know him and ask for permission to take me out.

While this may seem restrictive, my grandmother reminded me that as I got older, interest from boys would be more frequent and our family valued open communication. She, nor my parents, ever wanted there to be an opportunity where I didn't want to talk to them about certain things. Our family didn't keep secrets and we wanted to be open and honest with each other. We practiced this often so planning on my own was against our family's expectations.

My grandmother told my father about this interaction and on our ice cream drive that Sunday, he asked me about it. I was immediately anxious and didn't know what to say, but instead of being critical or disciplinary, he asked me one question. "How did that interaction make you feel?" Based on Grandmother's reaction about my plans with this boy, I knew that I was wrong, but it was my father's response that forced me to think beyond the butterflies I felt and look into my feelings. Then, I was able to see past the immediate validation of a boy liking me and take a moment to think about the implications of my conversation and plans with him.

At that same moment, I also realized just how much of a safe haven my father was for me. My family had high expectations, and I always knew that failure wasn't an option. But on that day, parked in that car, talking through the dynamics between boys and girls and safely exploring the decisions I had made and the feelings I had, I realized that this would be what family meant to me. That my father would always be my soft place to land, and that while holding me accountable, he'd always support my choices and respond to me with love and care.

Through accountability, my father's next question after we thoroughly talked about the situation was, "How will you respond now that you have communicated a plan with this boy?"

I didn't love the idea that I would have to go back on Sunday and tell this boy that if he wanted to spend time with me, he would have to meet with my parents and get to know them. I knew, however, that it was my job to do just that because I had made the decision and the plan. In that final question from my father, I learned that while my family will always love and support me, I was responsible for the consequences of my decisions and my actions. Having a strong foundation of support didn't absolve me of the outcomes of my choices. While there were many lessons that I learned from my father that day, with ice cream and a little bit of tough love, I realized just how important family was and would always be.

***

I often like to joke with my family that raising me was a team effort and I know that they agree. My father was strong and resilient and protective while my mother had a quiet confidence and strength. I call my mother my "heartbeat."

Professional Walk

Named after my grandmother Mozella, my mom was thoughtful in her words and never said more than needed to be said. But her words were always powerful. Sometimes in life you meet people who like to talk just to talk. That wasn't my mother. She was kind and thoughtful and supportive but also meant what she said. She had a strong sense of self and was unwavering in her belief in my brother and me. She could be outspoken when needed and reserved when her silence carried more weight.

I definitely gave my mother a run for her money in high school. While I was raised to be a respectful young lady, I was also taught to stand my ground and not take anything from anyone. I will never forget the first time I had to take that lesson in, firsthand. Best friends in high school can shift as often as the weather, but the first time I really had to stand up for myself was with someone who I considered my closest friend. This would also be the first person I would ever fight. My friend and I were coming back from P.E. class in our typical uniform of shorts and a t-shirt. I looked forward to getting back into the sweater my aunt had given me. I loved looking put together and I was known for always looking stylish. This sweater was one of a kind and no one else had it.

My aunt worked at Fortunoff in New York, so getting anything from her felt particularly special to a girl living in Florence, SC. This was a custom-made sweater that had my initials on the inside, and I was proud to show it off when I had the chance.

When the class was over, I went back to the locker room and my clothes weren't there. No matter where I looked, I couldn't find them. I began to panic, so my friend helped me look. We looked for quite a while, searching high and low, and in every nook and cranny that we could find. My clothes were nowhere in sight. Even though I was concerned, I had a feeling deep down inside that my clothes would have to show up again. I didn't know how long it would take, but I just knew that they would. To my surprise, my clothes would show up sooner rather than later.

The following week at school, I realized that my friend, and the only person who helped me look for my clothes, was the culprit. She had stolen my clothes and thought it would be a great idea to wait until the next week to wear them to school. I guess she thought I would have forgotten about my sweater by then, but that was definitely not the case. When she walked into the school wearing my clothes, I approached her. I'm not sure what she expected me to do when I saw her in my sweater, but she challenged me, dared me, not to say anything.

Because I was taught to stand my ground, I wasn't letting this go that easily. I wanted my clothes back and I was not going to be bullied by her, or anyone else for that matter. So, I had to prove to her and everyone else that I was not going to be taken advantage of. On that day, in the middle of the school yard, she and I fought. For me, it wasn't about the clothes; it was the principle of the matter. My friend had tried to challenge me and that bothered me to my core. She hadn't been truthful with me and if that meant I had to physically defend myself, so be it. I was strong minded and wanted to assert my presence. When my mother heard of this, though, I could tell she was disappointed. She was always so strong and unwavering. It was in that conversation with her, the day of my first fight, that she reminded me - I didn't have to respond in a physical manner to solve my problem. She said I was smart and had so much success ahead of me, but that fighting wasn't going to get me there.

I wish that I could say that was my last fight, but I will say that my mother continued to demonstrate strength through words, actions, and silence in a way that has stuck with me for the rest of my life. She always knew I had more in me. Even though she wondered if I'd ever graduate from high school because of my bold personality, she could always see my potential.

While many others thought I may have been stubborn or hardheaded, I viewed my high school years as a space I had to constantly defend myself. Like many small Southern towns, there is more to them than the charm you see on the surface. I was a dark-skinned Black girl and the oldest in my family. I was held to a high standard and wasn't allowed to fail. I felt I had to do everything right and anyone who attempted to keep me from that would be on the receiving end of my temper. I saw my fighting in school as a defense of my success. I was particularly involved in school and my community. I was in band, active in home economics, a part of Future Homemakers of America, and extremely active in my church. When others tried to bully me or treat me like I was less than, I took it personally and felt it was an afront to my potential.

In my family, school and church was our only job, and we were expected to do well. With all of those activities and expectations came pressure. While I didn't feel the pressure was beyond achievement, I did feel the need to perform, to be perfect. Couple those familial expectations with the ridicule of classmates for being the dark-skinned Black girl and you'll get the recipe for my defense mechanisms. While that included fighting at times, it also meant that my social circles looked very different. I tended to make friends with more boys than girls, and I often didn't go to social activities as frequently as my peers. Part of that was because I was so active in extra curriculars, but the true reason was that the friendships I created were a result of finding it hard to connect with girls my age.

I remember coming home from school one day and asking my grandma why I was dark-skinned. I was teased and made to think that there was something wrong with my skin tone. Of the friend groups I had growing up, I was always the dark-skinned one and as I got older, it was only more and more obvious that this wasn't desirable. My "friends" would tell me that I should bleach my skin and find a way to be lighter. In response to my question, my grandmother was taken aback. Although colorism wasn't foreign to her, having to talk to her granddaughter at such a young age about skin tones had to be saddening. I will never forget what she told me, though. She reminded me of my uncle, who is also dark-skinned, and that my skin tone was beautiful and natural. The most impactful thing that she said to me was, regardless of the challenges at hand, there is only one Rechel and that's all there ever will be. My presence in itself is beautiful, unique, and flawless because God doesn't make mistakes. She also told me that this doesn't mean that I am perfect but that I am pure in who I am and that I don't have to bleach my skin to be any more of who I was created to be.

It would still take many more years for me to fully embrace who I was and that I was one of the few dark-skinned people in my school. With this consistent support from my grandmother, I began to see the power within me and gave myself a nickname, "Dark n Lovely." I used this name anytime someone doubted, challenged, or tried to degrade me. I even put my nickname on the tags of my first car with an image of a coffee cup to remind people that you couldn't shake me. Ironically, I slowly became the girl that many girls wanted to be friends with. I was friends with a lot of guys who would also call me "Dark n Lovely," and their previous ridicule slowly turned into respect. I knew that I had to believe in myself more than anyone else and not allow the whispers of others to impact the view I had of myself.

Having my brother around also helped solidify the respect that people had for me. Although I was the oldest child, Richard always seemed to be my protector. He was outgoing and athletic and made friends wherever he went. Part of the reason I had so many guy friends was because Richard was such an extrovert and I naturally benefitted from that. I would describe myself as more reserved, but Richard always had a way of including me.

My brother was also smart. He is so good at math and money, and that has led him to be a great entrepreneur and businessman. Richard has always been a calculated risk taker. I was known for being in my books and focused on the path that is created for academically minded students, but that never really resonated with Richard. He knew he had what it took to be successful, but it was going to be on his own terms. We came from the same expectation in our family that failure was not an option, but our family knew that Richard was going to get there in a different way.

As a kid, though, that didn't matter to me. He was my brother, the social butterfly and the one who was always there to provide me with strength and optimism. While I was figuring out what it meant to be a woman and how to make friends, he was being a typical popular guy. He was a young, Black, boy in the south, so being the protector when we were together felt like his pride and responsibility. My father always talked about how I should be appreciated and respected by men, and my brother was the first one to show me this. In our adult years, Richard would help me through some of the toughest times in my life and often was the foundation for my success. He's never been one to judge me but always created space for me to find my own solutions.

With all of this support from my family and church community, I found myself holding up to a different standard than most my age. Yes, I did get in fights from time to time, but it was always steeped in my belief of self. My parents worked so hard to ensure that my brother and I had the best opportunities in life, and it was our job to engage in those opportunities with the best of ourselves.

Although I was more reserved, I commanded respect, just like my father. I was, and still am, outspoken and passionate about what I believe in. Through the challenges I saw my parents work through to provide a good life for us, I carried myself like I had everything I needed to be successful and truly believed that I did. My parents' love for us and their vision for our futures grounded me. I felt, and still feel, a strong obligation to be the best that I can be, and I found that my superpower was being fully me.

This perspective would continue to serve me throughout my life but as I graduated high school, I found out just how much those early lessons from my support system would prove to be invaluable. While my entire family thought that I would become a teacher, I was set on becoming a nurse. One of my first jobs was with Champus, which was a health care program. It was a temporary job that I had while embarking on my first year in college. It was a way for me to get started in my career and understand health care from different perspectives. In that time, my personal life was also thriving. I met a man who seemed to align with my family's values. He was slightly older than me and was a minister. I was still very involved in my church, and my spiritual life was important to me. This man seemed to meet all of the criteria for what I wanted, as well as the high standards of my family.

As we dated and started to fall in love with each other, we decided to move into an apartment together. During this time, I was managing the priorities of school, work, and now a love interest. We were starting to build a home, but the lasting impacts of my upbringing reminded me that I should be living my life in accordance with my values. So my boyfriend and I eloped.

When I reflect on that period of my life, I'm aware that it may seem out of character for a young Christian girl who is finding her way to elope with a man slightly older than her. It was, in fact, my Christian values and my strong ties to family and what it should be and look like that led me to this decision to get married quickly and without familial involvement. My newly minted husband was a minister and had a congregation to show an example to, and I always wanted to live a life that both my family and I could be proud of. On the surface, this decision seemed to make the most sense.

As we grounded ourselves in married life, I slowly began to see what my husband expected of me as a wife. Growing up in a traditional church home, many of these ideals made sense. I was expected to be submissive and yield to the authority of my husband as the leader of our home. My responsibilities included keeping the home in order through cleanliness and meal preparation. Eventually this would include childrearing.

Soon after we were married, I began to carry our first child, Antonio. At this time, I was still in school and working at Champus. My home life took on more structure as my son was born and the role in my family expanded to mother. My husband was adamant that I shouldn't work outside of the home and that he should be the breadwinner and provider.

While I didn't fully agree with this point of view, I quit my job and focused on school and our son. As a family, we attended church, I raised our child, and I continued on with school.

While I thought I was the image of a good and submissive wife, my husband disagreed and believed that I shouldn't be in school any longer. His idea of an ideal wife included sole focus on the home and family. I vehemently disagreed with this. I always saw myself as a woman with her own destiny, and I had planned to create a legacy of my own. I wanted this to include my husband and any children I had, but I didn't want my family life to eclipse all other aspects of life, especially my career.

This tension in our marriage led to a life that included verbal and physical abuse from my husband. Words of my father echoed in my mind surrounding how men should treat women. Scripture of what a husband and wife should be supplied my foundation, and while I knew I shouldn't be abused and controlled, it took time for me to distance myself from this relationship. In the meantime, I would become pregnant with my second child, our daughter, Brittany.

For the sake of myself and my children, I had to step outside of my ego and ask for help. It was my brother and father who helped me leave this relationship. I moved back home, and my parents and I discussed how I could move forward with my life. While my retelling of this part of my life is short, I must say that I have blocked out much of that part of my life. Aside from the birth of my children, this was a dark time. I felt I was doing all of the right things. I was going to church. I was married and had children. I took care of the home, and I wanted to give my family a great life through my studies at school. My hope was that this would yield a lucrative career that allowed me to live my wildest dreams. I relied on my upbringing in the church and my faith in Christ.

What I learned is that doing life the "right way" didn't mean that I wouldn't have challenges and tribulations along the way. At a young age, I knew that failure wasn't an option, yet I was in my early twenties with two children, an impending divorce, and living at home with my parents. This surely wasn't the life I had planned and now I was living it for more than just myself.

Throughout all of this, my family didn't allow me to feel like a failure. I was aware that hard things happen in life that can be out of your control, yet it's how you respond to those challenges that define your character. I was so thankful and blessed to have my family as my support system. This taught me that there is always someone to help you along the way, but you have to be willing to ask for it. I've always been a self-sufficient and strong-minded person. Asking for help when I felt I had failed in some ways was hard, but it reminded me that I do have support along the way. Having a village is not overrated and my success would depend just as much on me as it did my support system.

What I remember most about this time is that you don't have to stay in anything just because of the traditions outlined by society and the lessons you learned in childhood. My upbringing was a great guideline for living, but when life becomes gray and doesn't fit nicely into those lessons, you have to trust yourself and know what is right for you and your future. I learned that abuse doesn't equal love and that I can trust myself to do what is right for me and those that I care for.

What I've also learned about life is that things tend to work out, especially if you have faith. In an odd twist of fate, between my high school graduation and my divorce, I worked at my alma mater as an administrative assistant. When I walked through those doors, I remember feeling so comfortable. I liked the energy of the students, I enjoyed giving back to the educational space that molded me, and I was good at it.

Other staff members and teachers always commented on how organized and confident I was in the role. Sometimes they would mention the idea of teaching to me, but at the time, I was focused on nursing and wanted a career that was lucrative; I didn't view teaching as a way to make a good living. It's often said that if you want to make God laugh, show him your plans. I'd like to think this part of my life made him chuckle because in that same timeframe I had a unique opportunity to see how teaching could be as a profession.

My mother was interested in being a substitute teacher, and there was an exam that she had to take to qualify and be placed. As her exam approached, she had a scheduling conflict that she couldn't adjust. Being a frugal person, she didn't want to lose her non-refundable registration fee, so she told me to go in her place. I was skeptical and I hadn't had much time to study, but I went anyway.

I passed that exam and would sub at all levels of education, but mostly in elementary schools. I found that I excelled in the classroom. I had great command of classroom dynamics and was able to work through behavioral issues and cultivate a positive classroom culture. My students loved me, and I was especially adept at presenting the content in a way that the children could learn from. I had an "all-in" approach. That's always who I've been. I've always shown up with my full self and an attitude of success. Because of this, I started to become a highly requested substitute teacher and would be assigned long term substitute jobs.

Because of this experience, and after much conversation with my parents after my divorce, they agreed to help me in rearing my children so I could work and attend school full time, and eventually, find a job that would allow for stability. This time, I returned to school and changed my major to elementary education. I remembered my time in the classroom, and I was acutely aware of the additional responsibilities I had as a mother now. So, my life became school, work, and family. In that time, school often felt like a burden, mainly because I felt like a burden. The relationship with my ex-husband became bitter, and his involvement with the children became less and less. My mother and father stepped up and parented my children so I could get my affairs in order. This was a hard concept to acknowledge. I had to be selfish in my time with school and work so I could provide the best life possible for my children. I struggled with the idea that time away from my kids could in turn help them. This wasn't a part of the plan I envisioned for my life, but I knew I had to persist. I couldn't let those negative feelings hold me back from the life I, and my children, were meant to have.

When I graduated from Coker College with my degree, I'm confident that my peers had no idea that I had children or a full-time job. I had learned over those years to at least appear to have it all together. I often felt I had a lot of baggage and each step towards graduation would lighten my load. My degree isn't just mine, and the accomplishments from that time period are due to the support of my parents. I knew this next step in my life would set my family up for success, but there was no way I could really anticipate the challenges of this season being the foundational blueprint for the rest of my life.

CHAPTER TWO
The Belief

As a new graduate with hopes and dreams that I was ready to explore, I jumped into the job search with full force. I only had three requirements; one, I had to be close to my family - they were my support system, and I couldn't see my next stage of life without them; two, I had to make enough money to support my children and myself; and three, I had to be in a place that was safe.

I wrestled with the idea that I didn't want to stay in Florence but that most of my support was there. While Florence was my home, the place that helped mold me, it was also a place that held so many painful memories. I wanted a new start with new opportunities, and leaving Florence allowed me to feel I could leave those hard parts behind me as well. I kept my search local at first and looked in South Carolina. Unfortunately teaching jobs in South Carolina didn't meet my second requirement, money.

I knew that teaching wasn't known for being lucrative, but I needed access to enough money to support my children. I expanded my search to North Carolina. It was a few hours away from my family, but it seemed that there were more opportunities and higher pay just across the border.

I spoke with my family about it and while they were hesitant, they were supportive. After their blessing, I applied to job after job in Charlotte, North Carolina and started to get call backs for interviews. As I scheduled these, many of them ended up on one day. At that time, there wasn't a centralized interview location or online options, so I went to every school I was interviewing with. My parents went to Charlotte with me so we could tour the areas around the schools I was looking into, as well as see what living accommodations would best fit for my family and lifestyle.

At one of the schools I went to, the principal offered me a job on the spot. I wasn't expecting this offer so quickly and explained that I had other interviews that day. But he was resolute in his decision and said he could, "make those go away." He asked me directly that day, "Do you want this job?" In my research, I found that this school wasn't a very sought-after place to work nor in a safe area. Even with those factors, I immediately said "yes" and in that one day, I had secured my new foundation.

After that interview, my parents and I rode around town to look for places to live. We found an apartment fairly close to work so the commute wouldn't be far. The location was gated, and I felt safe to be there. It was close to stores, and I had a feeling that this would be a perfect start to my new life.

Upon my return to Florence, I prepared for the upcoming school year and my first year of teaching. During this time, I had many hard conversations with my family about what my life would look like now that I would be living and working in Charlotte. As I've shared, my family has been my rock and I couldn't have achieved as much without them. Over those years of work and school, however, my children had regarded my mother as if she were theirs. They knew that I was Mom, but my mother was Mom, too. My mother was that strength for us, and that included all of us. During those hard moments of my life, my mother always stepped into place for my children, and this would be another one of those times.

After much thought and discussion, my parents and I agreed that the best approach to my family's success would be for me to move to Charlotte by myself, at least in the beginning so I could build a strong foundation. I knew that I needed to get myself and my affairs together if I could ever reach the dreams I longed for, so I set off for Charlotte alone.

While my family wasn't far, I found that the miles between us served as the distance needed to initiate my healing and explore my identity. My children needed a mother that was happy and whole, and I needed to know who I was. I deserved as much. My kids deserved as much. This was a time to ignite my career and spend time finding out who I was. I am acutely aware that I could not have done what I did within those first two years had I been responsible for the daily care and rearing of my children. This time in my life *away* from them can only be defined by the motivation to do this *for* them. I felt like I had a new start and I wanted to 'make it right.' I felt like the life I was moving towards would be the life that I truly wanted and the life that my kids deserved.

As I began my first year of teaching, the classroom felt natural to me. I slipped back into my routine of classroom management, curriculum and learning, and creating strong relationships with my students. Thanks to my time as a substitute teacher and my education, I was able to be successful in the classroom and instilled a culture of excellence. It was known that I loved to teach with my door open, and although there were days that my door was closed due to safety measures, my preference was to keep an open environment in my classroom.

Professional Walk

On one of those days where my door was open, I remember being at the front of the classroom reviewing a passage that the students were reading. For some reason, I turned by back, and when I turned around, I noticed a gentleman sitting in the writing center at the back of the classroom. I didn't know who he was or why he was there, but I was not alarmed because he was a clean cut and nicely dressed man. There was a part of me that wanted to take a moment and ask why he was there, but something told me not to.

It wasn't uncommon for my classroom to have visitors. Sometimes this was due to classroom observations from administrators or visits from upper leadership at the district level, but my students knew that this was a norm. Staying on task and limiting distractions was a part of the culture of excellence my students had come to expect. They were not impacted by this visitor sitting at the back of my classroom, and while I noticed his presence, I did not acknowledge it. As I continued to teach, he was extremely engaged and didn't take his eyes off of me. Thankfully, my students stayed engaged in learning and our rhythm of that day's lesson continued. After about twenty or thirty minutes, this gentleman left without much interruption, and I later realized he had left a note where he was sitting. As I read it, I was surprised by the words staring back at me. Mr. Calvin Wallace had signed a note that said,

"You are an exceptional teacher who will not be teaching long."

While I appreciated the compliment, this wasn't a standard practice. I wasn't informed of any planned classroom observations, and this person wasn't someone I was familiar with. He didn't seem to be a parent of a student and the message he left was flattering but offered more questions than answers. I was hopeful that I would be able to ask my colleagues at a later time about that day's visitors to learn more about who was in my classroom that day. I wouldn't have to wait very long for my answer because as I was taking my class to the cafeteria later that same day, the assistant principal saw me and shared who that gentleman was. He told me that Mr. Wallace was a well-known administrator in the district and that he led the leadership academy. My assistant principal excitedly shared that Mr. Wallace was particularly impressed with me, and my mind wondered how he came to be in my classroom and what was so impressive to him.

I was always a very confident teacher and knew that I had a distinct skill for discipline and teaching method, but for someone to come into my classroom for such a short time and see such a clear vision of my leadership, I was particularly impacted. As time progressed, several colleagues would share with me that I had leadership potential. This was something that I had heard my entire life. In fact, when I was a child, I would often take the role of teacher. Not just in school yard games but even in how I related to my friends and my brother. My parents and grandmother would often catch me writing on furniture and walls, pretending that I was leading a classroom. It seemed like they always knew I would be a teacher, even when I hadn't considered it. And now, it seemed that the natural talent I had was showing through beyond the walls and doors of my classroom. Even beyond that, and as I was becoming more comfortable as a teacher, I was now hearing that my calling may take me to a level that I had never considered before.

To this day, I still don't know how Mr. Wallace ended up in my classroom other than my door being open and he found himself on my hallway. My faith teaches me that I am to remain steadfast in my spiritual relationship and that the desires of my heart will be realized. As an adult I learned that my calling was in education and I'm confident that the steps of Mr. Wallace were divinely ordered on that day.

A few weeks after seeing Mr. Wallace the first time, he visited my classroom again and recommended that I consider the leadership academy that he was leading. I was still a first year teacher, and this program was for those interested in administration. This path was a normal aspiration for a teacher in a long-term sense, but I was still getting used to being a full-time teacher. Considering an administrative role was nowhere on my radar. Ironically, the district I was in had rules against added duties for first year teachers, but I quickly realized that my principal didn't apply that guideline to me. I often heard that I was a "natural born leader," so I discussed this opportunity with my school's leadership. Over the remainder of that academic year, Mr. Wallace would continue to visit the school and discuss the many paths to leadership with me. Eventually, we exchanged numbers as I started to realize the major impact he could have on my career.

Mr. Wallace encouraged me throughout my first year and started to talk to me about taking on more responsibility at the school. As I entered my second year of teaching, I took his advice and started assisting at a middle school after-school program with a colleague of mine. I've found in my career that if you're willing to invest in yourself, others often will too. As I continued to engage in more and more opportunities, Mr. Wallace poured back into me. It seemed from the beginning that he could always see my potential, so our time together was always focused on my growth and ensuring that I knew the truth about administration and leadership in education.

Mr. Wallace led a leadership academy and while I wasn't in the program on paper, he met with me consistently to help prepare me for my next step. Each time we would meet for coffee, he would send me literature to read ahead of time. I was expected to review and analyze what he sent and think through the main themes and outcomes. In the meetings, we discussed what I thought about the literature, what I gleaned from it, and how I would apply it to my leadership. We often went through scenarios that I would most likely experience in my career, and we walked through the ways in which I should approach adversity.

Being such a new teacher, some of the knowledge he shared didn't always resonate with me in the moment. As my excitement grew for more opportunities to expand my career, Mr. Wallace would temper my expectations with the reality of leadership. He often reminded me that leadership was lonely and there would be many that would stand in opposition or ridicule every aspect of my decision making.

One lesson that has always stuck with me was that Mr. Wallace firmly believed that you were always interviewing for your job. This included the way that I dressed, when I showed up to work, and it seemed that the work clock started in the parking lot the minute I got out of my car. He expressed to me that as I grew in my career, there would be many who either wanted me to fail or believed I wouldn't be successful. To that end, he reminded me over and over that my job would always be open, and I should view any position that I was in as such. In our coffee sessions, he drilled into me that I'm always being watched and perceived and that I wouldn't always have the support of those around me. He underscored the fact that as I grew in my career, the focus of others would be squarely on me, and I would be assessed for a job that I may already have but could always lose.

I had dealt with hard things in my life and persevered towards success through many obstacles, so it was hard for me to understand what he meant by this. I had not only earned my position but did so quickly and excelled even faster once I had begun the role. I took on extra work and more responsibility when I had the chance and was often praised for the good work that I was doing. While I admired my mentor greatly, there were times in which I didn't agree with him or found his feedback hard to understand or accept. Hearing that I could be fired at any point and that my career could be lonely made me hesitant. While he was always supportive, I was used to being perceived as talented and exemplary, and I couldn't imagine having to be prepared for so much strife in my career. Additionally, I was on my own and building a life that would support my children when they finally joined me in Charlotte. Thinking about pursuing a career that was starting to sound less stable than initially planned, I had to take a moment to think through how I wanted to move forward. Being told that leading with excellence was always the expectation but that in doing so I would be consistently working myself out of a job was jarring.

Professional Walk

As my second year of teaching was coming to an end, my children came to live with me, and this felt like the beginning of another new phase in my life. I had two years to establish myself at the school I was teaching in and to accustom myself to the Charlotte area. I had taken on opportunities personally and professionally and had time to simply be, and become more of, myself. Once my children joined me, I would add after school activities like cheerleading, basketball, and track practices to my schedule. Making lunches, packing bookbags, and raising two young children became central to my life. I had to adjust my personal and professional life in a way that allowed us all to be successful.

I never lost sight of my career, though, and continued my meetings with Mr. Wallace. His lessons included topics that were tangible like how to prepare a memo or how to develop a schedule, yet, also included the softer skills like how to lead people and gain trust. I know that he deeply believed in me, and he told me as much. Even with that reassurance, I started to wonder more often how my time with my mentor had come to be. Yes, I had worked hard to differentiate myself and I leaned into being the best teacher and future leader that I could be, but there were moments of doubt along the way. The voices of my family always resounded in the back of my mind.

"You cannot fail."

"You are a born leader."

"You have to abide by your calling."

While there were moments that those reminders help steady my confidence, there were other times where I felt afraid that I could not reach all that was set before me. Mr. Wallace believed so much in my potential, yet he wasn't easy on me. There were many times in which I cried and struggled to see myself the way others did. I would ask myself, "Why me? Why so early in my career? Am I ready for this?" I had just been thrilled to get a job and not long into my first academic year I had a stranger taking me under his wing and teaching me lessons I sometimes felt too novice to learn. Hearing the weight of my potential future was overwhelming.

I was raised to be strong and faithful and often kept these emotions to myself. I didn't dare let others know or see me struggling with my inner voice. I never stopped meeting with Mr. Wallace, but I knew that my inner voice had to be quieted. I was consistently challenged, and I had to find an outlet for my doubt. Having been a person who journaled most of my life when I fell on hard times, I spent a lot of time writing about my experiences. There were nights after the kids were asleep and I was struggling to finish an article because my mind was too steeped in everything I couldn't see for myself, I would get quiet and write. I would talk to the pages of my journal and share the deepest insecurities that I felt. While the lined pages provided solace, I made sure not to stay there too long, so I also wrote down my hopes alongside my fears. I reminded myself of scriptures and embraced affirmations of my worthiness to do the things I was called to do. My passion was always children and their success, and I reminded myself that those children and their futures would rest upon the strong foundation that I was currently building, and that included the building of myself.

I can't say that I never shared my hesitations. There were a few times in which Mr. Wallace could tell that I was struggling or felt intimidated by the path set in front of me. These were the times where he provided tough love. He understood my perspective and my emotions, but he shared with me that my tears were just that, my tears. No one else would know what I felt and that my energy had to be focused on gaining resilience and growing tough skin. If I couldn't shift my focus away from my feelings and on to the calling, then I would not be a successful leader. If I couldn't do that, then I would be destined to be a teacher for the remainder of my career and the potential of becoming anything more would be fruitless. He saw greatness in me and his belief in me would only blossom through the investment of time and energy he gave. He was very clear that if I wanted to roll over and let the challenges overcome me, that I would be better off giving up now because I wouldn't make it otherwise.

Professional Walk

I pressed on over the next four years, but this conversation was not one that happened once and then I miraculously had the confidence I needed to succeed. On the days where I couldn't find the words to write in my journal to express how I was feeling, I just stared in the mirror. Sometimes with tears in my eyes, other times with steady streams down my face. If I could find words to say, they were shared only in the air between my eyes and the mirror; sometimes they hung thickly in the space between. Not providing comfort, just being. I had to learn to hold on to the unknown and remember who I was created to be. I had to remind myself of my foundation, my reasoning for all of this work, and continue to return to my faith. The list of those I felt I could not fail was long. My children. Mr. Wallace. My parents. Most importantly, myself.

Eventually, my skin got thicker, and my confidence became unwavering. I started to see what was happening around me. The list of those I didn't want to fail started to come into better focus and slowly reframed themselves as the list of those that wanted to see me succeed. Mr. Wallace wasn't just a person who wanted to see me do well, he was a deeply influential man within the district who was willing to spend his time and put his name on the line for me. His confidence in me was not out of kindness or emotion but out of years of experience in the field of education. His belief was steeped in expertise and practice. Calvin Wallace was highly respected, so if he was investing in me, people were going to take notice. Because of this, I was not being given any favors; I was proving myself to him. I learned that in this process, I was proving myself to me as well.

As I refined the thoughts in my mind and rewired my inner dialogue, the mirror that I once shared so many tears with started to hold my hopes more than my fears. I started writing on my mirror the things I wanted to believe about myself, and those things slowly became the things that I did believe, without any reminders. I was more intentional about the things that I read and took into my spirit. If it wasn't something education related, it would be something motivational; something that could ground me and push me further into the belief that I could achieve my dreams. Some read for pleasure or entertainment, but I knew if I was to be the best for myself and those that relied on me, I had to be specific about my growth and development. I couldn't allow for any distractions.

In addition to the content that I consumed, I also had to make some clear decisions about those I allowed around me. If you were not a person who was headed in the same direction that I was or could at least understand the journey I was on, I created a boundary. I was purposeful about my inner circle, and it had to be filled with those who offered reciprocal support and encouragement. If someone lacked the discipline and focus that I had, I couldn't afford to include them in my path towards my mission. I realized very early on that no one could accomplish my dreams for me, I had to do it myself. Those who wouldn't allow for my growth when in close relationship with me simply couldn't be along for my journey. I had to make a conscious effort to be protective of my relationships and the energy that had access to me. With this, I was reminded of the voices that I grew up with and were always there.

"You cannot fail."

"You are a born leader."

"You have to abide by your calling."

Those weren't going away but as I began to grow my confidence and strength, I started to add to them. They started to sound more like,

"You are bigger than your challenges."

"You have more potential than you can see."

"You have value."

The mirror and walls in my private bathroom were covered in encouraging phrases and quotes and in that space, I found a soft place to land when I needed extra momentum to get through the challenging times.

While I was building the scaffolding I needed to succeed, Mr. Wallace was alongside this journey and held me just as accountable. One of his primary questions to me would become, "What did you to today that got you closer to your goal?" He always asked this when we met for coffee, but he started to call me outside of those meetings and ask as well. This kept me focused on the vision that was set for my life. It wasn't enough to be prepared at our meetings through thoughts and conversation; I had to master concepts and execute. This preparation for leadership required me to show myself as worthy through action, not just through thoughts and intention. Although I felt the weight of this expectation, I had already decided that I wasn't going to let this process overpower me. I almost found myself in a mental game of, "fake it until you make it." I ensured that I was always prepared and laid the groundwork for my success, but in the moments that I didn't feel as confident as I needed, I sort of psyched myself out to believe that I could do the hard or challenging thing that I faced before I could actually do it. That is to say that I wired my mind in a way that the thought of failure didn't occur to me. I was so focused on what I could do that the idea of not being able to never crossed my mind. I was so resolute in my abilities that the idea of success became and conversation of when, not if.

So often, we invest a lot of time working to achieve our goals that when we start to reach them a fear of failure can set in. As I grew in myself and in the knowledge of education, leadership, and school administration, I learned that the fear of success could be just as jarring. Realizing your potential can be overwhelming and hard to digest. Seeing the dreams that existed in your mind turn into reality can be awe inspiring but also scary. I started to hear Mr. Wallace talk more about tangible growth in my career. During the years I would learn from him, I would become a teacher leader. and we started to talk about opportunities that would open up within the district in a way that was more structured and tangible than when we first began. The conversations we had shifted from theory to practice, and I started to walk beyond the early stage of my career with lessons that would be integral to my success at every future stage I would encounter.

Through those hard days and weeks of my time being mentored by Calvin Wallace, I learned that everyday could be a day of greatness, but that greatness had to start with me. I learned that, in tandem with my faith, I helped create my destiny. I had to be well studied and well prepared, and I had to show up to the table more organized, equipped, and informed than anyone else there. I walked through the halls of my school prepared to be the first one at meetings, the most suited to complete any task that required higher levels of leadership, and I always revered each day as another day to interview for my next opportunity. I fully embraced the phrase, "If you stay ready, you don't have to get ready."

The personal and internal work that I did in that time was deeply impactful, and I'm thankful for those who poured into me at that point in my career. But I can't forget that my faith served as a strong foundation for me when I didn't have the words or thoughts to understand what I was experiencing and feeling. Mr. Wallace often reminded me that those around me may not always be in support of me or be people I could trust. My faith reminded me that even leaning into my own understanding would inhibit my ability to grow in my calling. Scriptures reminded me that God was my sole provider and confidant and even as I grew in my confidence, my talent and potential resided solely in him. As my career progressed, there would be those who didn't want to move forward with me and thus didn't want to see me moving forward. In those moments, God was there to remind me of my walk. There would be many times that this walk consisted of only him and me. Through my experiences, I would come to know that there were even more times where the walk was just *him* carrying *me* through the journey.

As I continued to grow in my expertise and my aptitude, I was faced with those who didn't want to believe in me and my abilities. I had to learn to be true to myself. I had to learn that being true to me was the only responsibility that I *did* have. I couldn't base my worth on those around me, and especially not on those who would never believe in me to begin with. In the still moments of this season, I also relied on the words of my grandmother. My grandmother who was so strong and full of conviction. My grandmother who was specific about her words and intentional about her message. My grandmother who taught me that your words matter. You were to keep your words deliberate, concise, and impactful. That lesson served me well in my career. My words were always kind, but especially meaningful. I learned from her that you don't open your mouth unless you have something to say, and once you say what you have to, be done with it. This resounding message in my mind forced me to share my words with confidence and integrity, which allowed me to also be direct and concise. The words that I chose and the communication with which I used to interact with others allowed me to gain the respect and trust of my peers even when they may not have been a supporter. Coupled with my expertise and focus on growth and success, my colleagues, regardless of their personal feelings about me, could not deny my potential.

When we see the success of others, we can often underestimate the journey. We can assume that success comes easily to people, that they somehow have something that we lack or can't obtain. We often overestimate the inherent skills someone has. The reality is that achievement doesn't come easily. It is purposeful and the journey isn't a straight line. It is full of setbacks and valleys. There are low points when the goal or dream seems unreachable. There are high points where you can see the growth and distance you've traversed to achieve what you have. I will forever credit my future success to this stage of my life. I was able to make mistakes with a mentor who believed that I wasn't the sum of my downfalls. I would continue to experience challenges in my career, but this part of my life allowed me to grow the resiliency I would need to face those. I have been able to succeed in my career because of the belief: the belief others had in me, and the belief I was able to breed within myself.

CHAPTER THREE

The Promotion

There can be many ways to teach a concept. In the field of education, extensive research is conducted to learn more about how people learn. This research ranges from learning styles to learning techniques. It extends to deep research on neurological pathways and personality traits that are conducive to learning. There is even a research debate around what true learning consists of and is defined as. With all of that research, there will always come a time when the learning process isn't enough; there has to be a time of application. This allows learners, and teachers, to know the true extent of mastery.

As my mentorship meetings with Mr. Wallace continued, I knew there would come a time when I would have to show that I had truly learned what I was consuming and analyzing internally. I spent approximately four years with Mr. Wallace on a consistent basis. In those four years, I was teaching in the classroom and over time, I engaged in an afterschool program that was led by a colleague of mine. I wanted to participate in any opportunity that allowed me to apply the knowledge and skills I was learning. I was able to become a teacher leader in my role with my employer, but that role was still based on carrying out initiatives and decisions made at the administration level. I wanted the opportunity to step into the more integral parts of being an administrator.

I didn't lead the afterschool program, but I was given responsibilities that allowed me to be in a leadership position, guiding six to seven people. As my responsibilities and successes grew, I learned that people were increasingly interested in what I had to offer. Simultaneously, I was finding myself becoming more and more confident in the possibility that I could step into leadership and administration. The concepts I was learning through my reading and mentorship were being utilized in practice, and I was becoming more comfortable with the idea of where my career could grow. To this point, my career trajectory existed only in my mind. Through my time with the afterschool program, I felt the thoughts in my head were becoming tangible experiences that pushed me to grow deeper into my potential.

With this renewed sense of direction, I started to have conversations about more formal leadership positions and started a master's degree in Educational Leadership. I was learning how to trust myself and become firm in the impact I could make within the field, and I was ready to show others as well. Through those conversations and starting my degree, I was able to transition from my teaching role to an assistant to the principal role. This new position would give me an in-depth perspective into the school and district level system. While I wasn't able to formally sign off on policies, procedures, and discipline, I could carry them out, and I was a part of the discussions that would define those initiatives. I was excited to see what would be required of me and have the chance to show that I could rise to the challenge. I didn't know then what a challenge it would be.

Through my professional experiences, I was confident that I could conduct trainings and teach others how to facilitate learning. I could go into a school and model what to do in a classroom. I could show you what the components of a well-planned lesson were. I could help you create an assessment that would truly tell you if a standard or objective was mastered by your students. I could even teach you about the unfavorable parts of teaching, like how to be a great disciplinarian. Unfortunately, that's not what this role needed from me. I now had to do all of those things with people who didn't want to do that with me. I was used to being the trusted expert in those areas, but now I was having to gain trust from those who didn't have a belief in me.

Some colleagues felt I was too young and inexperienced to have any impact or knowledge on their work. Some thought that their way of doing something was not only the right way but the way it had always been done. Who was I to come in and think I could change anything? Who was I to think that my way was better? Gaining trust from people who had been doing their jobs for 15 or 20 years and getting them to understand and believe my vision was a particular challenge, one that I was having a hard time overcoming. This part of my role was so challenging that it was the first time I realized that leadership might be more than I bargained for.

In prior moments of low confidence or adversity, I was being poured in to by my support system and I had positive reinforcement that I was good at what I did. But what happens when so many others don't feel the same? I would always have my support system, but this was the first time I was being faced with dissent in my abilities. I would soon learn that it wouldn't be the last, but this forced me to adjust my approach. It was no longer enough to be good at something. I had to engage others in a vision that they may oppose, and I had to gain not only their trust but their belief and energy to carry out the goal.

While trying to expand my leadership style to gain support, I found that I also had to be silent about the experiences I was facing and the feelings that came along with them. I may have been working with people who didn't believe in me and made that clear, but I couldn't respond to those outwardly. I still had to smile and be helpful. Finding peace in my journal yet again, I kept coming back to the question, "How do you help someone who doesn't want to be helped?"

There were many times when I couldn't understand how I could be seeing an educator fail, that it was clear that they weren't successful in their methods, yet they still didn't want to change. It seemed rooted in their comfort and the amount of time they had been doing things their way. They were committed to the approach that made them feel comfortable and stable, even if it wasn't serving their students and causing them great frustration. It seemed easy to observe that while they may be comfortable in their style of teaching, they would in turn be frustrated by the lack of student success or their student's behavior and attitudes towards learning. I found that many teachers were unwilling to change their practice but still wanted exemplary outcomes.

Although the frustrations of those teachers didn't make sense to me, I realized that they weren't going to change because I said to or because I felt strongly that they could do things differently. That wasn't leadership. I wasn't leading anyone just because I held the radio; that simply made me someone who was carrying the radio. This was the part of leadership that I did not know. This wasn't the part that was in the literature that I was reading or in the scenarios that I was working through in my mentorship meetings. This was the part of leadership that was the unknown, and I had to put in work to find what this part of leadership would be for me.

I wish I was able to say that I effortlessly learned this part of management, but I can't. If you asked me how I did it, I would say through experiences and trial and error. I hit a lot of walls. I had many times where I had to go back to the drawing board because my first or second try didn't work. And I want to be clear, sometimes those failed attempts bred more challenges. When I tried something that didn't work, those I was trying to lead became more resentful and rebellious. Sometimes my failures in leadership created more distrust in my abilities, so I then had to regain confidence of others as well as still accomplish the intended goal.

Those moments were hard and at the core of it all were students who needed to have the opportunity to succeed. Everything that my colleagues and I were doing was for them, and I couldn't let the trials in my leadership journey stray from that fact. I still had to smile and be professional, even when I knew my colleagues didn't care for me. I had to continually show up and provide support to them without resentment and frustration. Even when I thought this person would be better off in a different profession, I still had to maintain positive regard for their potential and find ways to support their growth and development. It's what the children deserved, and it's what my leadership required.

The dissonance between what I was feeling and how I had to show up in my work was particularly hard. I was never one to be fake or show myself as one thing and be another. I struggled to see leadership as a path that required me to be dishonest with myself to succeed. I never wanted to be the type of person or leader who engaged in the politics of the education system or the workplace. I would soon find that an added layer of relationships and connections would impact my work. Sometimes those who I found to be most problematic had relationships with leaders and influencers within the education system. Sometimes these teachers and administrators had strong ties to the community, and anything I did would take on a life of its own, beyond the task at hand. I had to traverse the balance in accountability and the political landscape of the environment that I was in.

At times, I was encouraged to overlook poor behavior because it would be easier if I just waited until they retired or found another position. I realized that this approach to accountability was standard practice. I was expected to let things go because others felt that it would better serve me. I knew that this was not going to be my attitude towards leadership, so I started to prepare myself to go against the grain. I knew that the challenges I was experiencing would only be complicated by my decision to remain ethical, so I started to arm myself.

As I stepped deeper into my resolve, I began to feel the ridicule of my fellow administrators. Those who said they were there to support me were the very ones who stood against me as I tried to remain true to my integrity and aligned with a mission to improve education for our students. I realized very quickly that I was supported until I hit a nerve, until I was holding people who administrators liked, accountable.

In this role, the words of Mr. Wallace rang truer than I wanted to admit, leadership was lonely. I didn't understand the full weight of those words until I found myself disliked for the things so core to my leadership. My passion. My expertise. My values. I had seen leaders make poor decisions before and receive the consequences of those actions, but I hadn't considered being disliked and unsupported for doing what I felt was right. I didn't think I'd be disliked for staying true to the core of my profession and keeping the students and children at the heart of my decisions. Knowing that I was remaining true to myself and the calling helped ease the feelings of loneliness and struggle, but it was still hard to process.

Leadership forced me to make tough decisions and still choose to lead from a place of love and care, even when that was not reciprocated. On the days when I didn't want to deal with the tensions, I remembered why I was there and who I was there to serve. There were many days that I couldn't stand to hear my name and didn't want to deal with the challenges of the day. At times, it felt like all of the problems of the school were saved just for me, placed on my doorstep to handle. I was committed to ensuring our children learned in environments that would not be a detriment to them and their success, so I still had to answer the call, especially when I didn't want to or felt overwhelmed by the expectation. I had to become bolder in my resolve. The decisions I made had to be ones that I could live with, ones that allowed me to sleep at night.

I knew that I didn't have the support of everyone that I served through my leadership, so I had to be a leader who didn't have to look over my shoulder and worry if the choices I made would contribute to my downfall. I had to stand tall in what I believed and keep the mission at my core. I had to learn to make decisions that I didn't need to apologize for. I made decisions that I was confident that I would have made again and again if I had to do them over. I knew that I wanted to be known for my character and my integrity, and I would only be able to do that if I made decisions that I could stand by, regardless of how unpopular they may have been.

Professional Walk

It may sound noble or even obvious to stay true to your values, but it was surprising to learn just how fragile a career in education could be. When Mr. Wallace reminded me time and again that I was always interviewing for my job and that I couldn't be afraid of being fired, I found out how true those words could be in real time. Making decisions that I could stand by was easy compared to the mental preparation I had to undertake when I wasn't confident that a decision would prove positive for my career. I found myself making decisions that many people didn't like and beyond their feelings about me, I ran the risk of not being invited back the next academic year. Working in education isn't just about making your direct supervisor happy. You were evaluated on the school's success, on the work of the teachers you oversaw, and in the public opinion which includes parents, community members, and local leaders. The scope of impact could not be underestimated, and it challenged me to be that much more attuned to my value system.

Because of the public nature of my role and the outcomes of the choices I made, I had to adopt a few guidelines that protected me from those who didn't have my best interest in mind. I quickly realized that there were people who would agree with me to my face but would have differing opinions when I wasn't around. Through this, I learned that if I wasn't in a discussion or a meeting where something was said, I had to treat it as if it didn't occur. I felt that I had to be guarded about who I could trust and intentional about how I responded to information that was shared with me. Unfortunately, I found that my female colleagues were more often my opposition and that felt particularly hurtful. It reminded me of the times in high school where I had to constantly defend who I was and had to make sure no one was going to disrespect me in the process.

I remember feeling especially disappointed that the women I shared my career with were the ones who created barriers and obstacles for me. Being a Black woman in the South, you grow up knowing that you'll have to prove your worthiness and skill to those who don't look like you. I had childhood experiences with racism and sexism that told me that I couldn't fail, yet it would be harder for me to succeed than any other group. Knowing this didn't make me feel good, but at least I knew the parameters set in front of me and was aware that they would be there.

I was taken aback when I found that the barriers to my success would come from those who did look like me. From those who may have wanted what I wanted. And, from those who couldn't see that they could have what I had, while I also had it. I didn't believe that there was only a certain amount of success to go around and that you had to fight for what little there was. I believed that we all could thrive and be successful in our own right. This dynamic reminded me of high school but unlike high school, physical fighting wouldn't resolve my issues. I had to learn to ask questions, to open dialogue rather than assert my dominance just because I had a title. In fact, it became a well-known fact that Ms. Anderson wasn't going to just take your word on anything, she was always going to ask if you wanted to talk about it. Some took issue with this, but it allowed me the opportunity to parse out what was real and what was a motivation at play. I learned that I couldn't take anything at face value, and I ensured that I held myself accountable to fully identify and consider the underlying forces present when leading others.

I am thankful that I learned how to deal with those who felt threatened by me early on in my career, but I've remained disappointed in this type of behavior throughout my career. Within this first leadership role is where I learned to put a wall up around me and created a space where I trusted no one. I believed I had to do this because anyone I interacted with had the potential to "set me up" to see how I would respond in any given moment. I felt I had to stay on my toes at all times and the sooner I protected myself from any opportunity to fail, the more likely I was to succeed. It wasn't something that I accepted easily, but I realized that this was what I said "yes" to.

With this guard up, I learned to show up every day with consistency and reliability. I needed my actions, my thought processes, and my decision making to speak for me when I wasn't in the room. I didn't deviate from the way that I responded and what I responded to. This allowed people to know how I would approach my work and where I stood on issues facing our school and our students. I remained humble and thoughtful, but consistency remained my priority. There were a few losses I experienced along the way, but I had to be okay with that. Every battle I interacted with was not there for me to win, yet it was there for me to address.

I had to accept that I wasn't going to win against every obstacle that I encountered and that 'winning' wasn't always an indication of success. I had to reframe success as, first, showing up, and then giving it my best. When I would reflect on how I faced those obstacles, I would ask myself a set of questions that I felt guided my leadership from a place of character and integrity. I would ask,

> "Given the same circumstances, would you do the same thing again and for the same reasons?"
>
> "If the consequences of your decision negatively impacted someone you loved, would you stand by your decision?"
>
> "Did you limit the amount of hurt caused to others?"

Professional Walk

"Did you leave everyone with their dignity?"

If I could answer those questions from a place of sincerity, then I knew I had made the right decision. I knew that I couldn't lead only from a place of expertise and knowledge; I had to be reflective in this process so I would continue to grow. I knew that if I was to be the leader I intended to be, I had to do so by being able to answer those questions honestly and consistently. As I began answering those questions over and over with every decision that I made, I noticed that my skin became thicker, and my internal voice became tougher. I was less and less rattled by the challenges I was experiencing because I knew that I could stand by the choices I made, and I could deal with any consequences that resulted.

As I became a stronger leader, I started to define success differently. My focus shifted from what people thought about me to what people knew they could expect from me. I was less concerned about being perceived as "touchy/feely" and more concerned about being known for being fair and true. I was perceived as someone who was tough yet fair, and someone who was always clear about what she stood for. I wanted my legacy and reputation to be one that allowed people to see my core motivations and want to work for me, with me, or hire me because they knew I would always be true to the best intentions of the profession.

Professional Walk

Defining what success meant for myself, not based upon anyone else's definition, was the game changer. This would be the guidepost throughout my career and continues to serve me even today. This was especially helpful when I found out that the funding for my role, assistant to the principal, had run out. It was in the middle of the academic year, and I was told that there was no more money to continue this role. I felt defeated. Mr. Wallace assisted me in finding a place to land, a fourth-grade class to finish out the year, but I felt I had failed. For all of those people who doubted me and felt that I didn't have what it took to succeed, I, for a moment, believed that there may have been something correct about that.

I had stepped into this role as I was starting my masters and as I was meeting consistently with Mr. Wallace. I knew that I still had steppingstones to traverse, but I felt I was on the right track at the right time. What would it mean that I had spent the past year and a half gaining the trust of those who didn't, and didn't want to, believe in me just to return to the classroom alongside them? Although I would be teaching at a different school than I was leading in, my ego was still bruised. I knew that I had to walk through the halls with my head high, even if my confidence was shaken. I didn't want this setback to define my career, but I didn't see any other opportunities for me to prevail.

Within my time in this role, I felt so aligned with my purpose. I was doing quite well in school, and I knew that the culmination of this hard work would result in the accomplishment of a dream. Not only would it allow me a better paying position to best support my family, but I would be gaining a career that I loved. This degree and this position would get me to the next level of my career, and it served as a great model to my children that we can do hard things and still achieve our dreams. During this time my children and I were always focused on our success and growth. I was proud that I could show my children that although life wasn't perfect and that you would come across hardships, you can, and should, persevere to attain your goal.

At the same time, being in school allowed me to have peers who were focused on the same things and had similar aspirations. They were just as hopeful as I was that we could be principals and beyond if that was our goal. Those peers also helped me stay grounded and focused because they were sharing the experiences they were having at their schools, and it bolstered the fact that leadership and this journey was hard for everyone. It was what you had inside of you that would make the difference. All of this helped me build the strength that I needed and reminded me that I didn't have to be perfect or have all of the answers.

Professional Walk

As long as I was willing to grow, it would be easier for me to not internalize the difficulties I was facing and having peers who understood helped normalize my experiences. So, when I had to take what seemed like a step back in my career, I did so with more knowledge and preparation than before. I still had to press forward and remain grounded in the principles I had defined for myself. I couldn't let my children see that this was bad for our family; I had to show them what overcoming could look like. In the midst of confusion, they would see that I sucked it up and continued to do what was right.

I walked in to that fourth-grade classroom with every intention of serving those students as if they were my own children. They were going to get the best from me, regardless of how I was feeling about my career. As I prepared myself to return to the classroom, I was able to put what I had learned about leadership back into the context of teaching in real time. I also learned that you can't put all of your eggs in one basket. You have to remain nimble and plan for the "what ifs" in life.

My fourth-grade class was available because it was supposedly one of the worst classes within that school. It had run many teachers away, and the students were not doing well on the state assessments. I knew what I was capable of, so I was intent on not running away from them. I finished out the school year with those students achieving higher test scores, passing their subject matter successfully, and a part of the overall success of the school. Although I was so disappointed that I had to return to teaching for that short time, I realized by the end of that year that my purpose is pre-destined, but how I show up, is what I control. I didn't let the embarrassment or the discontent I felt hinder my ability to excel in any environment. I knew that I was an effective teacher, so I embraced the path that I was on, regardless of the circumstances.

Once I finished the academic year with that fourth-grade class, I had to figure out my next step. I finished my master's degree and I couldn't go back to the school I was the assistant to the principal at because all positions were filled, even for teachers. Months prior to the end of the year when I returned to the classroom, I remember asking Mr. Wallace why he would have even encouraged me to take on that leadership role. I remember asking him, "Why did you do this *to* me?" He told me very succinctly, "Because you're strong enough to know what to do."

It didn't make sense to me at the time, and I didn't really know what he meant. But at the end of the school year, he had seen me adjust to my surroundings and succeed. I was set on ensuring that no one saw me sweat or struggle, and that included Mr. Wallace. People were looking at me to see what I was going to do next, so I did what I knew how to, succeed. I needed to adjust quickly and make sure that I didn't lose sight of the long-term goal. I'm so very thankful for that experience in retrospect because I think this "setback" was exactly what Mr. Wallace needed to see to recommend me for the next step in my career.

I was essentially unemployed by the time the summer came along, and I needed to find my next opportunity. Mr. Wallace knew of a principalship at a private elementary school, and he believed that I was ready for it. Once he told me about the position, I was hesitant because I only had experience in public schools, but I applied anyway. I had to interview and prove my value to this small, suburban, religious private school, but I knew Mr. Wallace would give me a great recommendation alongside my credentials. I finished the required employment process and was found to be the final and selected candidate. This was yet another point in my career that I would step into the unknown with hopes that I would be successful.

As I prepared myself for this role, I took with me the lessons that I learned through the first five years of my career. I had worked hard to identify my goals, set targets and work to execute those. I would need that same tenacity in this new role. I knew that I was walking into a principalship with less experience than others might have, so I had to balance being open to learning and growth, while also asserting the leadership skills that I did have. I had learned the value of gaining the trust of others, especially of those who didn't believe in me. I knew I'd have to employ those skills again.

The most important lesson that I wanted to carry with me was that I had to also be in a place where I could live with myself and the decisions that I made. I knew that if no one else cared, that I had to be the one who did. I couldn't give up or run away when things were hard or didn't go my way. I had to be strong in my convictions and stay the course when I brushed up against challenges. At the time of my transition to the principalship position, I found myself thankful that I had such demanding experiences because I don't think I would have felt prepared or aware enough of the environments that I would soon experience in my next position.

CHAPTER FOUR

The Principalship

There is a common phrase often used when you embrace a new experience with hope and joy but also naivety: "You don't know what you don't know." I felt ready to level up my career and walk confidently into a principalship role, but I knew that this new environment was different than anything I had experienced before. I was used to urban, public schools, and my first appointment as a principal was going to be at a suburban, private, religious elementary school. I had spent the previous few years gaining knowledge and understanding of school leadership, but I knew that there would be a learning curve.

Mr. Wallace's belief in me and my potential helped keep me grounded when I felt the weight of doubt as I thought about this new stage of my career. I had transitioned out of my role in the classroom and the principal who I was under while being a teacher was retiring. This felt like divine alignment, and I was ready for the shift, but I was nervous. I thought that a small, rural, private school might be a great place to "get my feet wet." I knew that my experience as an assistant principal wasn't enough and changing from being someone under the decision maker to the final decision maker was intimidating. I would soon learn that the level of expectation and stress would increase, and I would have to be more intentional than ever about my leadership journey.

Since my childhood, I always had an eye for doing things myself, for myself. While I loved the opportunity to grow under leaders in my career, I always had a yearning to be more entrepreneurial and prove that I was as talented as I thought I was. This first step into a principalship would be my time to learn just how prepared and capable I was. Throughout my first year, I learned many tangible skills, like how to interview for quality staff members and what to do when programs weren't successful. I also learned more about making decisions about curriculum that would be best for students and how to build consensus and collegiality in the workplace. I had spent a good part of my career being intentional about boundaries at work because I didn't always have people rooting for me, but this role challenged me to be thoughtful about the relationships I decided to build.

As the final decision maker, I also had to be well studied and prepared. So many people were looking to me to lead this school into success, and I had to be confident and assured every time I walked into a room, regardless of the context. This school was tied to a religious congregation as well, so I quickly learned that community there would consist of parents and teachers but also parishioners and community members. This was a major adjustment compared to my previous experience, and there were many times when I wondered how any one person could do all of this. It often felt I had to be perfect in every facet of my work and personal life, as so much was being asked and expected of me. I had to find a new balance at this level of leadership to be successful. I had learned the balance of leading under someone as well as following, but this level of expectation was very new to me and took more effort to achieve.

As I worked through my first year, I realized that the shift in culture and expectation wasn't in alignment with my core values and principals. I also learned through this experience that knowing what doesn't align with you is just as important as knowing what does. Walking into this role, I was excited for something new and aware that it would be a substantial growth opportunity, but I also felt like it was an imposed next step. I had risen to an assistant principal role yet had to return to the classroom due to circumstances beyond my control. I wanted to continue growing in my career, and this opportunity was one of the few that were available. While at times this opportunity felt divinely ordained, at other points I felt obligated through circumstance. In this new culture and environment, I felt I was at a crossroads in a career that I hadn't felt was in alignment with my previous experiences and purpose, and I struggled.

Being a part of an educational environment that was so closely tied to religious belief and the church community meant that everyone had a specific opinion about how the school should be run, as well as the entitlement to share those opinions. The political landscape of the church had deep impacts on the operations of the school, and it was challenging to navigate what was best for the students and work within the confines of the culture. I also felt immense pressure to succeed when Mr. Wallace had put his name out there to support me in this role. I wanted to do well for him, my students, and the family I had to support. I learned quickly that I had to "go with the flow" if I was going to succeed.

I loved being the principal with an opportunity to strengthen broken processes and build them up again. I liked putting my own spin on things and the process of trying new initiatives to see if they made a positive difference. I loved building up my staff and helping them learn and excel. Most of all, I loved my students and the good work that was happening for their success. What I didn't like were the hoops I had to jump through when interacting with people who had thoughts on my leadership direction and decisions without a knowledge base or expertise in education. At times, it felt the school was created for parishioners to have an option for their children to learn at a place that they trusted to have the same religious values they were accustomed to, that they had input in, and could afford. This culture created a feeling of community for parents and students but stifled exposure to difference.

I remembered walking into my school and often thinking about how this wasn't my home church and that I had little interest in being within that community religiously, but the community wanted me there. Not just at the school but in the church on Sundays, and there was an expectation of high visibility. While I showed up and honored my commitment, I felt it was out of duty and necessity due to my need for employment and support for my family. I learned quickly that it wasn't enough to have a passion for education and my students, I had to align with the culture and environment, and this one wasn't for me. I wanted to be a leader, but not in this type of setting.

As I came to realize the nuances of my own professional values, I reflected on how this position would integrate into my career trajectory. There was a perception that principals within the private sector had a lot more opportunity and privilege to lead an environment they had a lot of choice over. I was able to choose my own staff, resources, and curriculum. While I was leading a team with complex cultural expectations, the structure of the environment didn't seem conducive to my future goals. In the public education system, you had to learn to work with what you had and make hard decisions. There were, and are, positives and negatives to each environment, but as I refined my preferences, I noticed that it got harder day by day to lead in a school that didn't "seem like me." I took this role because I wanted to move to a higher leadership position and scope, but this was not the leader I had decided to be when I joined the profession.

During this time in my life, I really struggled with the desire to be myself and be a great leader. I didn't want to compromise myself for a position, and it felt that this role required it. I had to shut down a side of me. I was no longer Rechel; I was simply the principal they needed at the time because no one else was in the role. It was at this time that I had to decide the type of leader that I was going to be in an environment that I didn't enjoy and also how I was going to pivot and learn what I needed to so I could then move to another position.

The balance of perspectives and wants from a deeply involved community forced me to learn not to take things personally and not to beat myself up over the feedback I was receiving. It seemed every day there was a new complaint or source of feedback, and there was always the threat of someone "going to the pastor" in an effort to have more control over the operations of the school. I learned that I simply couldn't be all things to all people, and I had to prioritize what the day to day would look like. I had to shift focus often and I learned to be nimble and flexible. Everyone comes from their own perspectives, and while I honored the thoughts of the school community, I had to remember that my perspective, coupled with my expertise, was also valuable. I learned to not focus so much on the individual feedback that I was hearing and to instead concentrate on the broader outlook. I couldn't think of just one child; I had to think of the entire school.

At that time, I was still very young in my career and experience and was concerned about losing my job. It took some time to cultivate the courage to make decisions and stick beside them when I was in an environment that others felt so comfortable openly criticizing. I also realized that when I tried to be all things to everyone, I lost sight of the true purpose, the children. As I reset my vision on the success of my students, I started to strengthen my boundaries and remembered the power of my 'no.' I wasn't nasty or biting, but I was clear and firm. I had to be a situational leader and that required me to re-strategize often. My core purpose stayed the same, but I had to be adaptable enough to adjust to my audience, the demands at the time, and the priorities of the school and its success.

With this new empowerment came a sense of calm over my future. Knowing that I was standing by what I believed in took the sting out of the threat of being fired. If that would ever come to be, I could be satisfied that I was true to myself and my purpose. While it may take some people a while to realize what they like and don't like within an environment, I am happy that I was always an intuitive and fast learner. I was in this position for one year and knowing within two to three months what was working for me and what wasn't helped me adjust accordingly for the remainder of the academic year. I also had to learn quickly because I was no longer under someone to learn the 'ins and outs' of a school. I had to learn it on my own and occasionally consult with my mentor. A lot of my learning came from my conversations with Mr. Wallace, and I went through a lot of trial and error.

I would like to be certain that I flawlessly found a way to navigate this challenging environment, but that's simply not true. There were times where I made some poor choices, simply because I didn't know better. The benefit of that was my learning continued on through the poor decisions and outcomes, and I was able to learn for the next time. I would have loved to have been perfect, but since I am not, and wasn't at the time either, I found a way to focus on the learning of this process rather than the disappointments that came with some of the consequences of my leadership.

One thing that I found particularly helpful was focusing on the facts and separating myself from the emotions of decisions. Because I was always so focused on learning, I once again returned to the subject matter. What were leaders in the field doing in practice? What were the theories of education saying about some of the things I was experiencing in my school? I came to the school environment with knowledge and support of my decisions, and this lessened the burden of making tough calls. I knew I had the expertise and insight needed to make a sound decision, and I used that to my benefit. I still listened and observed, but I now had a well-studied filter for which I could sift all of these inputs through.

As I became more comfortable standing in my own power, I also decided that I needed to pivot to a new role for the next academic year. I started the search process early, as I didn't want to miss an opportunity. I wanted to return to the public sector and get back into the system I was formally in. Although some thought my private school experience wasn't transferrable, I was able to navigate my interviews in a way that I could express the context of my role and its environment as well as showcase my leadership abilities and relevant skillset. Regardless of the stereotypes of private education, I knew I had learned an abundance in that role, and I was intentional about continuing my leadership journey in the public-school environment.

I interviewed for, and earned, an assistant principal position and was excited to transition back to a familiar environment. I was happy to get out of my current school, but I did wonder what others would think about me moving from a private school principalship to an assistant principal position in a public school. I wondered if some people thought I wasn't able to handle leading a public school, and I reflected on how this move might impact my career. I didn't want this to be something that would hurt me later. The school I was transitioning to was not as affluent as the private school, and it was a middle school, not an elementary school. It was one of the toughest middle schools in the district because it faced rising crime in the neighborhood while dealing with gentrification at the same time. The original culture of the community was fading out and a different culture was coming in and erasing the legacy that was already there. It was a challenging environment for those students and a hard school to work in, and it was the best experience that I could have ever had.

***

Professional Walk

It seemed I had gone from one extreme to the other in terms of environment. If there were hard knocks, that school had them. I remember receiving my last check from the private school and feeling so confident in the future of my career and my decision to move back to a school and system that really aligned with my soul. There were many times when family and friends asked, "Are you going to be okay over there?" but I felt so assured that I had made the right decision. I would grow to really love that school and the work I was able to do there, even as an assistant principal. I had been so worried about the next steps in my career, but this school reminded me of why I did this work, why I wanted to be in education in the first place.

Make no misunderstanding, though, this was a tough school to serve as an administrator. There were all walks of life represented. There were varying levels of poverty and some gang activity. The staff knew that many kids were carrying weapons and gang paraphernalia to both protect and defend themselves, and we also knew that there was a particular culture that surrounded the school environment where students thought that was a needed component to attend school. For many of these students, school was not a high priority, and there was a lot of trust building that I had to engage in to still have an effective learning environment. This is where I found the most joy. Helping students see the value in their education and the hope education could provide brought out the passion in me. This was a challenge I hadn't experienced yet, and I loved learning how to navigate it.

At the private school, I turned to learning and research and books to be well studied. In that particular community, I needed proof that I knew what I was talking about and that my decisions were grounded in something. I had to prove my worth through knowledge. At this school, I quickly learned that it didn't matter how much I knew, who knew that I knew it, or how well I could do the administrative work of the job. What mattered here, what my success was dependent on, was whether or not I was viewed as a leader who cared about people. I could move mountains if people knew that I cared about them. Once the students and parents knew that I cared, they were willing to take the journey with me towards success and growth. It took all those prior years of experience to realize that everything I consumed to learn and grow my knowledge had to be coupled with care. I couldn't have one without the other if I wanted to be a leader that had impact.

I spent three years at this school, and it taught me how to build something from nothing. Some thought I couldn't handle this position because I was taking a step down from a principalship. Others thought that I was overqualified based on my previous experience. I thought that every experience I had until that point culminated to this. I had all the makings of a leader, but I hadn't yet put it together and it was at this school where I had fertile ground to do just that. There were days I left broken and unsettled about my leadership and this role; there were other times where I felt challenged and much better for it. I realized that as I grew professionally, so did my understanding of success and the value of never counting myself out. I learned to maneuver around hurdles and still have a successful outcome. I learned how to be a good proxy for my principal and gain the trust and respect of others. I learned that while I may have had the qualifications by title, I didn't have the experience I needed to be the best leader I could be.

I find this sentiment to be true in many people's careers. Often, we can be focused on 'moving up the ladder' and less on the experiences we're having and the learning that is occurring. We can be solely concentrated on the position, the trajectory, the pay, and the accolades. But what happens when we get to the destination but can't remember the journey? This assistant principalship may have challenged my ego, but what I gained in turn was invaluable. I'm confident it was a turning point in my career so I could step into the fullness of my potential.

I have always viewed myself as a builder. I come in and assess the landscape, think through the issues, come up with the solutions, and execute. I've seen this as a strength in my career. I'm a fixer. I was known for working with struggling students, curriculums, or schools and helping them get to success. Once the goal was reached, I felt I had fulfilled my legacy and I was ready to move on. In my assistant principalship at the middle school, I was working with eighth grade students. They were the last stop in middle school and this group was the largest at the school. An opportunity to be an assistant principal at the feeder high school became available as my beloved eighth grade students would be transitioning there, and it felt natural to go with them. I was able to secure that position and move up with my students. I had a relationship with so many of them, and I was particularly invested in their future. I knew that I could help them graduate high school and I wanted the opportunity to do so.

While the high school itself was new, the environment there wasn't dissimilar to my previous experience at the middle school. I felt a level of confidence because of this and felt I had the basics down. What I didn't plan for was how different high school would be. To this point, my career focused on K-8; this was high school. Things were different and so was the focus of education. There were two ways that high school could prepare a student, for the workforce or for college. Instead of focusing on the next level of education and making sure students were ready to go to the next grade, being a leader in a high school meant that you had to prepare these students, these young adults, for the world. The level of accountability on the student and the staff increased and shifted my work from nurturing kids to instilling confidence and self-sufficiency in young adults.

In addition to the change in expectations, I also found the professional environment to be different. It was far more competitive. It seemed like every assistant principal was vying for the principalship, and I became acutely aware of every decision I made. This broadened my mindset to not just the work that I did and the success that I had but how I fit into the overall structure. I quickly realized that because of the competitive environment, every move I made was observed and scrutinized. I also learned how to consider many different perspectives on my actions because there were that many eyes on me.

This time in my life reminded me of the political landscape of my private school principalship. Although it was my colleagues this time, the themes seemed to be similar. I have never been one to be political. I like to be authentic to myself and true to my values. I haven't spent much time in my career wondering about the power structures of education. I believed that if I did a good enough job, I would have that work rewarded in time with the ability to move up in my career and learn more. While that may be my value system, it was clear to me that I was working with colleagues who differed from that. I had to be thoughtful about how to approach my career in this landscape and still be true to myself.

I decided to remain true to my mission but work harder to gain the trust of my colleagues and administration while also standing out for the good work that I was doing. Although it was hard, I also wanted to be intentional about giving myself grace. I allowed myself to fail, to make space for trial and error, and to not hold myself accountable to perfection. I also had to learn to let time have its way. I watched my colleagues 'race to the top,' and I had to re-center myself and remember my faith in God and his timing. What I thought should happen in my career and the timeline in which it happened couldn't be up to me, and I had to remind myself of the principles I learned in church to encourage me when I saw things happening for others when I felt they weren't happening for me.

I was able to be successful in this school with students, but this was a challenging professional environment. It took time to establish myself and my value to the school. I had many successes along the way, but I had to be mindful of the political and power dynamics at play and not take my journey too seriously. I had to continuously re-commit myself to my true purpose, so I didn't get caught up in the pressure to join the 'rat race.' Although I spent an abundance of time thinking about my faith and being faithful, I built up a wall around myself. I felt this would be protection from those who were hyper focused on their career and would do anything they could to get there. I wanted to gain the trust of others but was very hesitant to lend them that trust in kind. I saw what people would do to excel and stand out amongst the rest, and it made me hesitant to build personal and professional relationships with those I worked alongside.

As I continued in this school, I learned that I was deeply trusted in the area of discipline. I had always been an educator who commanded respect from students, and I held them accountable. I strongly believed, and still do, that accountability is akin to love and care and is integral to a student's success. Many people in this profession don't like this aspect of their jobs. I can understand why but it seems that I have been particularly gifted in this area, so although I was competing with others for the opportunity to move forward in my career, they trusted me to be a leader in the area of student discipline. I recognized that this was solely because they didn't want to do it, but it was a great space for me to shine without much interference. At the same time while I was able to stand out in that arena, it was clear to me that opportunities that may have had more value to administration were being withheld from me.

Finding a balance between my natural strengths and what was deemed as valuable to the system was a challenge. I was doing great work, but the work I was doing didn't allow for the opportunity to have the influence I needed to rise to the next level in my career. I started to work on intentionality in my trust developing skills. I was specific with who I gave bids for trust to and for those I felt I couldn't trust, or for those who felt they couldn't trust me, I focused on respect. If I couldn't have a mutually trusting relationship with some people, I needed, at the least, their respect. My work ethic and genuine interest in children and their success helped me forge those respectful relationships, and this began to shift the paradigm.

Working hard to shift the perspective to my work ethic and respect also pushed me to move the focus away from my personality and myself and on to the work. I was always going to be confident in who I was and what I stood for, so there was no need to think about adapting aspects of my core personality. What I could focus on was the work, the success, and the school. I lead my colleagues to do this with me as well. I had to do so subtly, but when I found myself being challenged due to a personality conflict, I always refocused on the work. I was further able to do this because I didn't leave much room for anything other than work. I came in early, stayed late, and made sure to be outside of my office and in the school environment as much as possible. Unless there was a student in my office, I was visible within the school and took a lot of initiative. I helped others and volunteered for the things that people didn't want to do. I fully immersed myself in the organization so when people saw the school, it was easy to associate it with me as well.

As I began to gain buy in from my colleagues, I was simultaneously increasing favor and bolstering support from my mentor, Mr. Wallace. He was seeing my growth and development in real time, and it seemed that as he saw my commitment grow, his support in me grew as well. I think he always believed in me, but he wasn't going to invest more into my future than I was willing to invest in myself. As he saw me get more and more serious about doing good work in my career, he became even more committed to my success. I started to see how people began to view me and my potential and as that reputation grew, so did my aspirations. I felt I was ready to prepare for my next level up, and I enrolled in a doctoral program. At this time, my two children were in school but getting closer to their own high school graduation. In many ways, it was reminiscent of my master's program where I was doing homework alongside them.

What's interesting about my decision to go back to graduate school is that, in my mind, I was preparing to step out on my own. My sights weren't on a principalship anymore. While I wanted to stand out and have a strong reputation in the field of education, the competition at my current job reminded me just how much I wanted to be out on my own. I wasn't sure what that would look like quite yet, but I knew it would be in my future and on the horizon. I also knew that I'd have to have a few more leadership roles within the school system before becoming an educational entrepreneur. I would need to feel prepared, and respected, enough in the field to accomplish this. When I thought about those next steps, I set my sights on district level roles, primarily in curriculum development. I was also open to teaching about K-12 education at the college level, so enrolling in a doctoral program seemed to align with where my destiny seemed to lead.

I remember being so excited to enroll in classes. I loved learning, and I felt I was really embracing my career once again. I felt invigorated and ready to take the role of student again. I was at the high school when I received the acceptance letter, and I experienced a full circle moment. I was going back to school to better pour into the educational system I was literally standing in. I called my mom and read the letter to her. In a school with 2700 students, it was very busy, and I think she could hear that through the phone. I'm not sure if it was the loudness of my life, or the history of that same life, but she was happy, yet hesitant. She had seen me push through a lot in my life and keenly remembered helping me care for my children when I first went back to school after my divorce.

My children were older now, but they still had a lot going on. They were involved in all the things most teenagers are and I was working a lot. Could I take on more? How would I balance it? What would support from her and my family look like? These were all valid concerns for her, and for me, but I was focused on continued improvement and viewed this as yet another opportunity to support my family, to build on her legacy. This time, my children were with me. I mean this quite literally; they attended the school where I worked. This level of integration helped me feel that I could do this. My son would later transfer to a different high school before graduating, but at the time it felt the pieces were all falling into place. Soon after I received my acceptance letter and prepared my mind to reenter the classroom as a student, Gardner Webb called to welcome me over the phone. Not only did I have this letter to mark this new journey, but I could now hear the weight of my next journey in the voices of my future instructors.

Because my children were young adults, it was easier to manage my many responsibilities between work, family, and school. My children could make their breakfast, get themselves ready in the mornings, and jump in the car with me to go to school. They could start their homework on their own and manage their social calendars. It wasn't easy, but it was manageable. I also had the support of my family as well. When my son chose to transfer to a different high school, that made my life a bit more complex. He couldn't jump in the car with me and go to school anymore; we weren't going to the same place anymore. This made mornings more complicated and scheduled. Thankfully, my brother, always one of my biggest supporters, bought my son his first car, and with that blessing he was able to drive himself to his new school. It was moments of support like this that I credit much of my success during that time to.

As independent and strong willed as I was, I once again had to be reminded of the importance of a village of supporters. No success occurs alone, no matter how alone you may feel or how independent you may be. Within my school I had to learn to be skeptical about who I trusted and that naturally raised walls and barriers to letting others in. In an effort to keep people out, I was also shutting off an opportunity to let support in. The doctoral journey isn't an easy one, and I didn't realize the amount of construction I would have to do to the walls I had so strongly fortified.

During this time, I also realized what my mother was so nervous about. The organized and accomplishment focused side of me felt proud that I was keeping all of the wheels turning. I hadn't dropped any balls and I was doing well in my classes. I was doing homework alongside my kids, and we were in this together. What I didn't realize at the time is that the time I was spending with my children wasn't of quality. It was rooted in routine and most of the time we were together was focused on checking off the boxes of the day. We weren't connecting. In that time of our lives, it was a far cry from the ice cream drives on Sundays of my childhood.

That part of my parenting was missing. I was accomplishing the things that I needed to on the surface, but I was missing the opportunities to make memories with my children. It was also during this time that I was building my first home. I wanted the best for my family. I ensured that it was in a great neighborhood, that the home itself was better than anything we'd lived in before, and that my children would participate in any thing they wanted because it was in a place where they could thrive. I was so focused on what I thought was the perfect life for my family that I missed some of the core things needed to be true of a family--time, energy, and love.

While there were some mistakes along the way in this part of my life, I will never neglect the nuances of my mindset. I don't think I was a bad mother for wanting these things for my children; however, when I reflect back on my life and career, from where I'm standing today, I would have done it a bit differently. I would have realized that the cost of my degree and career aspirations weren't paid only in tuition and fees, but in time away from my children. None of us can use money to pay for love, care, and relationships. We pay for those things with our hearts. With our time. With our energy. Without realizing it, I would soon come to recognize just how impactful the time missed in those years were. As my kids started to graduate high school and enroll in college, my studies were still in full force, and I had been at the high school as an assistant principal for a few years now. I was feeling more and more established, and as I interacted with my peers in my doctoral program, I was feeling more confident than ever that what I was experiencing in the workplace wasn't uncommon. I could see myself growing and learning, and I felt great about my station in life.

There is an old adage that says, "The only constant thing in life is change." Just as I was feeling secure in this phase of my life, my grandmother passed away. Grandma Mozella was one of my biggest supporters and so influential to my life. The grieving of her death was overwhelming. I could feel myself sinking into a place that I didn't recognize. There were many days when I didn't want to, and couldn't, move forward. I did only what I needed to in order to keep my job and meet my financial responsibilities. School was hard for me. I could muster up the energy to go to classes but studying independently was hard. My brother saw that grandmother's death had a deeply negative impact on my life and often found himself consoling and encouraging me. He felt I had worked so hard for the successes I had accomplished and knew that my grandmother wouldn't want me to give up simply because she wasn't with us anymore; she would still want me to continue on.

Right before my grandmother had passed, Mr. Wallace talked to me about putting myself out there professionally and encouraged me to think about looking for a principalship position. Because my children were getting out of the house and starting their adult lives, this made sense to me. I applied to many positions and looked beyond North Carolina for employment. I applied and interviewed and was denied many times. As I continued applying and interviewing, Mr. Wallace was there every step of the way, reminding me that professional growth included accepting disappointments. I was used to 'acing' interviews, and it didn't seem like many opportunities were working out. Through every 'no' I received, though, I learned how to brush myself off and hold my head high. I also learned that a 'no' could also mean that those positions weren't the right fit for me. 'Nos' could be good, even helpful, in finding the right fit.

Because of the timeline of applying for jobs and the death of my grandmother, I found myself moving to South Carolina for a new job as a principal at a K-5 elementary school and trying to figure out how to balance school with the memory of my grandmother at every turn. I had such a swirl of emotions. I was excited for a principal position at a school that I felt aligned with my purpose. I was so sad because I didn't have my grandmother there to share it with me. I was stressed because I was behind in school and didn't know how to get back on track. I was anxious because I was embarking on so many unknowns at one time, and it was overwhelming.

Professional Walk

As I settled in South Carolina, and at the constant encouragement and support of my brother, I reached out to my dissertation chair and set a plan to complete my degree. Because I had changed schools and my research was focused on the school where I was previously employed, I had to adjust many aspects of my dissertation. This added another year and more money to my already stressful life. My brother told me that if I committed to finishing, he would pay for my tuition. He knew how much this meant to me and how much I knew it would mean to my grandmother. I was back on track with a plan for school and in a new position that I was hopeful would let me use all that I was learning to lead students to success.

In this job, I was coming into it with grief, and reflection, and I think this gave birth to the beginnings of me setting better boundaries at work. Being contemplative about the life of someone you have lost forces you to consider the life you're currently living. What was most obvious to me at this time was the amount of life I wasn't living because I was so focused on my goals. These goals and accomplishments built the life I was living now, but the most I could think about was time spent with my children and those I loved. I hadn't considered dating or having much of a social life. I thought my grandmother had a great life and I wanted to ensure that I was living mine as fully as possible.

Professional Walk

I tried to be intentional within this new role while still giving myself grace. This was hard at times. I remember one night in particular that has always stuck with me. I was in the library and really struggling with my research. Although I had a new plan to succeed, I was considering quitting. That isn't a foreign concept to a doctoral student, and the thought of quitting occurs as a sort of commonplace rather than an outlier. On this day I was struggling to find reference material within the timeframe I needed. Every source I came across was either too old or not quite what I was looking for. I wasn't analyzing data or writing a chapter for my dissertation; I was simply trying to find relevant sources. That was supposed to be the easy part and for some reason, it was feeling difficult.

A wave of emotion and frustration come over me. I wanted to cry, and quit, and be done with it all. In that moment, I could hear my grandmother Mozella so clearly. I could hear her voice saying, "Pull yourself together. You already have everything you need." What was odd is that her voice was as clear as crystal, and I honestly believe it was her. This voice was not me speaking to myself because I felt her presence, and I felt her support. I had an emotional moment thinking about my grandmother watching me struggle in that library, doubting myself and forgetting what she had taught me. I couldn't let anything get in the way of my promise, and that included getting out of my own way. It was as if she was sitting next to me, telling me to go get what I needed and then to get over myself. In the few minutes I listened to her voice and words of wisdom, a sort of calm confidence washed over me and I was renewed. I knew that although my grandmother wasn't there for me physically, she was surely there in spirit. Her belief in me wasn't any less because she couldn't be there with me in the flesh.

It must have been divine energy. That night I was able to refocus and not only find the sources I needed, but I wrote some of the best quality pages I ever had. From that night on, I was able to remind myself that I would not be beaten by hard things. As anyone who has worked on a dissertation can attest to, there are many moments when you are challenged and come up against hurdles you didn't foresee. That night in the library is one of the most impactful reasons I was able to complete my doctoral degree. The diploma may have had my name on it, but my grandmother's name was written in the fine print.

Coming back to South Carolina afforded me the opportunity to be closer to my family and visit more often. The school was in a rural district and a part of a small community. It was the first principalship I'd held at a public school, so even though I was going through trials in my personal life, I still placed a lot of pressure on myself to do well. I thought that this was finally the time I could make my mark in a school that aligned with my professional values. I was excited, yet I quickly learned that the environment I just moved to was very different from the environment I had just come from. I was used to a large urban community with more resources. I still came from a public system that needed funding, but being at this small, rural school highlighted just how many resources were lacking. I remembered walking the halls of the school over the summer and thinking about how dim and dark they seemed. I wanted my school to be colorful and bright; I wanted it to be a place where learning was fun and motivating.

When I asked for the funding to buy paint, I was told that it wasn't in the budget. I immediately thought that this couldn't be true. There was no way a school could not afford a few gallons of paint as well as painters. How was I supposed to make a difference when the resources were so limited? How was this going to impact my students? In education, I was used to doing more with less, but this seemed extreme. I reached out to Mr. Wallace for advice. I was feeling discouraged and unsure if I had made the right decision. He said to me very plainly, "You will get the principalship that's for you, so this is for you." He reminded me that my feelings had little to do with the potential of this school's success and the potential for my leadership. I was reminded that the skills needed for this role were already within me.

Professional Walk

If I walked away from the opportunity to lead this school simply because it didn't look like what I thought it should, that would mean that I was walking away from those students, from myself, and from my career. So, similar to what my grandmother would have told me if she were alive, I got over myself. I started to think about what it would take to make my vision come to life. I wasn't going to let the lack of budget limit these students. I started to build relationships over the summer. I got out into the community and connected with the staff, teachers, and parents. I shared my vision with enthusiasm and the belief that I could make it happen. Some looked at me with confusion and disbelief, but there were others who I could see were bought in to the ideas that I had. While I was out getting to know people within the community, I met a family of painters and carpenters. I immediately felt lucky and shared my thoughts with them about how much the surrounding environment impacted the success of children and their learning. The family responded excitedly and volunteered to help paint the school before the academic year started. I was ecstatic.

In looking at the budget, I had just enough to buy the paint needed. This family painted the school for free. I worked in partnership with them. I didn't just count my blessings, I rolled up my sleeves as well. I scrubbed walls, pulled staples out of surfaces, applied painters' tape, and secured all of the materials they needed. I fed them while we worked together, and I was so grateful for this opportunity to not only transform our school but also to build relationships with them. We worked on the school in the mornings and after hours as well as on the weekends. It was a true labor of love and by the time school was to start, the students were walking into a clean and safe building that welcomed them and their potential.

If it wasn't for the 'real talk' of Mr. Wallace and my prior experiences in building relationships and vision setting, I'm sure that this school would have looked the same as it did when I first walked in. This made for an amazing kick off to the year. Everyone commented on how this academic year 'just felt different' from the prior year, and it seemed to be a place where people wanted to be again. Although I wasn't there the year before, it seemed that there was a shift in the mindset of the students and staff. In a matter of two months, I had made an impact so great that building support and trust for my future decisions wasn't hard. People knew that I was deeply invested in this school and community from the start, so they were happy to be on board.

I had found a school that finally connected with my purpose. In this role, I found my challenges were less around getting people to believe I was worthy of their followership and more around exceeding my goals each year. In my first year, I was able to make a literal transformation to the school, so how would I continue to capitalize on these successes? Within that first year, I was awarded Principal of the Year, so the pressure to excel was of particular importance. When I find myself in moments of decision making, I try to get quiet with my journal. Over the years, my journal had been my most trusted life partner and this point in my life was no different. I started to strategize what I wanted my time at this school, and in this district, to look like. As I've mentioned before, I was known as a fixer, so my plan was never to be at a school for more than five years. I thought about what the next three to five years would look like for this school under my leadership. As I carved out what year two would look like, I thought about the metrics of success and how this school could get on track with performance and outshine prior years.

Trying to outperform yourself year after year is a worthy goal and is a valuable effort, but this drive, coupled with my personality and slant towards achievement, forced me into my old habits of overworking myself. At this time in my life, I was in a mindset that was between two norms of living. I wanted to be successful and career-driven, but I also knew that being solely focused on my career wouldn't allow me to truly live life. I always had a lot of support from my family and because I was in South Carolina and close to my hometown, I was able to visit my parents and brother often. On a few of those visits home, I reconnected with an old friend, and we started dating.

It had been a long time since I was romantically involved with anyone and after my marriage ended, it was hard to learn to trust again. Reconnecting with someone I already knew and someone who was a friend to me years prior made me feel that I could let down my guard and try to embrace the softer sides of life, the parts of life that didn't have to be protected. In time, I would become engaged to this person and we would have a child together.

A child is always a blessing; however, I was a single, female principal in a rural area. I was deeply concerned about what people would think of an unwed mother leading their school. I held myself to a high level of accountability, and I wasn't sure how this would impact my life. Having a child was so far from my reality. In fact, when I was experiencing symptoms, I was sure it was everything under the sun other than pregnancy. I went to my primary doctor and was just sure that I was having issues with my blood pressure due to stress. My doctor mentioned the possibility of pregnancy, and I was adamant that this wasn't possible. Not only was that not in the plans but I was using birth control. I was confident that I was being safe and protecting myself from this outcome. My doctor suggested that I take a test to rule it out. When the test came back positive, it took almost an hour to calm down.

I sat in that waiting room in amazement and confusion. I had so many thoughts running through my head. In the days and weeks that followed and as reality set in, I began to think about how this pregnancy was no longer personal. I was a public figure now, and this was an area of leadership that I hadn't considered. Yes, my career had impacted my personal life for many years, but I wasn't used to my personal life having an impact on my career. Not in this way at least. Unfortunately, there were many whispers about who the father was and how this happened. I was always a relatively private person when it came to my personal life, so to have a part of my life on display for others to judge was just plain hard. More than that, I had to be careful about my health during this time. Due to my high blood pressure, my pregnancy was considered a high-risk. Many times before I had tried to live a balanced life, but this pregnancy required it. I could no longer think about making a change to find more time to live life; this baby needed a mother who would be devoted to her and put her first.

To this day I still say that my daughter, Erin, saved my life. When I was pregnant with my first two children, I was in a dark place. I was in an unhappy marriage, and I was young. I didn't have anything figured out, and I was trying my best. I relied on my family, and the start of my parenthood journey didn't look the way I thought it would. Although Erin was a surprise, I had an opportunity to approach motherhood differently. I was financially established, I had a stable career, and I was much wiser. I felt far more confident that I could provide for my child, and I embraced this unexpected journey openly. I started to adjust my way of life and created boundaries between my work and personal life. I didn't stay late or arrive early as often as before, yet, I was still highly engaged. This meant that I was intentional about cutting out distractions and procrastination at work. I had to show up for Erin, so that meant I had to truly learn to delegate. Delegating isn't always easy, and this challenged me to fortify that skill. Trust is a large part of delegation, and I had trained myself to remove opportunities for disappointments at work. I never wanted anyone to have an opportunity to make me look bad, but now I had to trust others to do a good job with the work I was giving them. In the end this was a much-needed skill and allowed others to grow in their careers by having more responsibility, but it was hard.

As I was working hard to be a great mother and a strong principal, I also had to deal with the mental stress that came with juggling it all. At that point in my life, I remember struggling most with the perception others had of me being a working mom. I knew that I wanted Erin's upbringing to be different than Antonio's and Brittany's, but I had to learn how to be okay with what others would think about that. I felt I was being judged, and I didn't like the pressure of that judgement. At the same time, my relationship with Erin's father was ending, and although we didn't get married, we were still good co-parents. As life evolved and I came to experience more events that I couldn't control, I started to adjust my expectations around caring what others thought. I had to re-center my focus on the health of my child and the quality time we spent together. Erin compelled me to start living my life on my terms, and I became more and more resolute in that with every passing day.

I was firmly in my third year at this school when I realized that I was ready for a change. I didn't want to stay for five years. I thought I had done great work in my three years there, and I wanted to start looking for opportunities. There were a few dynamics that were happening behind the scenes that were attempting to challenge my ethics and integrity, and I felt that it would be best if I moved on. I've learned in my career that knowing when to leave a position is an exceptional skill, and it can help you maintain a positive reputation. It's always better to leave on top. It took some time to find opportunities to move on. As I was moving up in my career, openings for other principalships or district level positions were infrequent. Of course, there were less of these positions than entry level roles, so I had to strategize when thinking through my job search. It was another year or so before I was able to find another position and, in that time, I would learn a valuable lesson.

I had so much life happen in the three years at this school. I had high levels of success and another child. I was truly enjoying my time and when I was ready to leave, I thought I'd be leaving a strong legacy behind with lifelong connections as well. In my fourth year, this all changed. I shared with my leadership that I planned to leave at the end of the academic year for another position and my environment completely changed. People who I thought supported me unwaveringly were cold and hard towards me. It made me wonder if the relationships I formed had been disingenuous from the start. I'm not sure if people were simply upset or if they felt betrayed by my moving on, but it was clear that they weren't supportive of my choice. I found my time at work to be less favorable than prior years, and I didn't feel that I had the support I needed to finish the year strong. I was saddened that I was being honest and transparent in an effort to help this school find the next right person for my replacement. Instead, I was met with disdain. Quite honestly, it was nothing less than painful, and as I completed the academic year, I left feeling unhappy and unsupported.

In the end, I had to do what was right for me and while I suffered some unpleasantries, I knew that I had made the right decision for my family and me. I had to be okay with my choices and this one felt right. I learned through that time that I can't control what other people think or do, but I don't have to engage in it. I made it a priority to continue to treat people with respect and dignity and was intent on ensuring that my behavior never wavered, even in the face of those who did. At the end of the school year, I said "goodbye" to my students and while it was sad, I knew that I was a part of their success story. In my closing remarks at our end of year ceremony, I remember telling them that although I was leaving as their principal, I planned to be back as their superintendent. I'm not sure what compelled me to say that as I wasn't planning on becoming a superintendent, but maybe it was the doubts I saw on the faces of those who once supported me. I knew that I had made a marked difference on this school, and I wanted them to know that my devotion was just as strong as it was when I first stepped onto campus. If I knew then what I know now, I would have known just how true the power of the tongue is.

***

When we go through tough things, most of us hold onto hope that it will yield something good and worthwhile on the other side of the struggle. I was surprised at the treatment I received when I left my elementary school, so I had a mixture of emotions going into my second principalship in the public sector. I was transitioning to a middle school that needed some care, and I thought it was a great opportunity. This would be my third principalship overall, and I felt ready to take on this new academic year. I was hopeful yet feeling a bit scarred from the last position. I was also coming to this position with a young child and bolder boundaries. I wanted a different environment in which I could thrive in all areas of my life. I was happy to learn that this experience would be exactly what I was looking for. I was reminded of my time in Charlotte, North Carolina when I was an assistant principal at a middle school. This school was in Marion County, so it was less rural than where I had just left but not quite as urban as Charlotte.

I had been in a middle school before, and I felt that I had an array of leadership experiences to pull from. So, I was confident. Once I was in the role, the staff was supportive yet hesitant. They would often mention that it was a challenging environment and would say things like, "you must not know where you are" when I would make suggestions for growth. It's true that I have always been ambitious in setting goals, but I also knew where I had been and what I'd overcome. My new staff didn't know my capabilities, but I was happy to have their support, regardless of their doubts.

I knew that I was coming into an established environment, so I set out to make relationships right away. That came easily. In fact, this position was the most pleasant role I had to date. I went into this experience expecting challenges and planned to approach them with the confidence of my expertise and qualifications. In this role, I also found that I had an extremely supportive superintendent and deputy superintendent. This seemed to make all the difference in my level of growth and success. The leaders I worked for were hands on but not micro-managers. They had an open-door policy, and I was welcomed to ask questions. It was clear that they wanted me to be successful, and their goal was to provide me with the support that I needed.

It was in working with them that I started to consider what it might be like to be a superintendent. I hadn't given it much thought until then. I finally saw a superintendent that I wanted to be emulate one day. I remember thinking that these were the role models I needed to see myself in. With each opportunity to learn and grow, the idea of such a large role seemed less daunting. I was given constructive feedback and even when I made mistakes, my voice was still valued. It was under their leadership that I realized you could have a high level of responsibility and still not be perfect. That wasn't the job. The job was to create and refine systems that helped students succeed. It wasn't about the accomplishments of yourself but those of your district. The role required that you pour back into those you were leading and that really resonated with me.

If I could help teachers be better teachers, and students have more success, that would be deeply connected to my life's purpose. I didn't realize that I needed to see this career path as a possibility until I had. In my mind, I found superintendent positions as fraught with politics and time spent managing public expectations, not true change in the education system. I learned and grew in an environment that felt genuine, and it allowed me to open myself up to areas of vulnerability that I would need to strengthen if I were to seriously consider this next step. The leadership at the time made me feel they hired me to do a job that they knew I could do, and I wanted to return the empowerment and support I was receiving to my colleagues and future leaders. Seeing their example would be the springboard for my new career goal: becoming a superintendent.

CHAPTER FIVE

The Superintendency

It's amazing how your life can blossom when you have the support you need to grow. When I think about the teenage girl who felt the need to fight her way towards respect, I wonder now how light her burden would be if she felt supported and accepted from the start. I spent a lot of my life baring the weight of proving my value and merit. As I journeyed through my career, I recognize that I spent much of it trying to make others see how qualified I was to do the work I was already doing. I spent years building relationships and working tirelessly so others could see that I was worthy of the positions I was in.

Professional Walk

When I moved to Marion County and had leaders who not only supported me but valued my voice and decisions, a different part of me and my leadership style awakened. I didn't have to spend energy on convincing others to trust me or the decisions I was making. This allowed me to focus on the work and fine tune the areas in which I needed to grow. I approached my work holistically and didn't have to concern myself with the dynamics of relationship building. I was trusted to do the job I was hired to do, and more than that, I was expected to do well because my leaders knew that I could and would.

I started to move with a deep-seated confidence that seemed to bloom greater than it had before. I was being poured in to by those who were dedicated to my success. I spent three years as the principal at that school when I saw a Director of Curriculum and Instruction position open at the district level. Unlike times prior, I wasn't hesitant to apply and more importantly, I was confident that I could do this job. I had the thought of becoming a superintendent now firmly rooted in my mind, and I thought that a role at the district level could be a great opportunity to level up my skillset and understand leadership from a broader perspective. I spoke with my deputy superintendent about the role and received support.

With that additional push to apply, I did so and was selected. As I transitioned into this new position, I was able to intimately see what it meant to be a leader at this level. I came into this role very easily and found myself to be a quick learner. Curriculum and Instruction was a passion for me, and I had a vested interest. It wasn't long after, though, that my dissertation chair noticed that I had outgrown the role. As I met with Dr. Kathi Gibson (my dissertation chair, mentor, and encourager), she made note that I didn't seem passionate about what I was talking about when I discussed my job, and she told me very directly that I should look for the next point in my career. I hadn't been in this position long, so I was surprised by this feedback. I knew that I was bored, but I wasn't sure if it was the job or that time in the academic year. I had just gotten into the role and Dr. Gibson was telling me to move on.

In reflecting on my mindset at that time in my life, I felt the sum of my experiences had prepared me for where I was then. I felt I was an ordinary person who had moments that provided extraordinary growth and opportunity. It was in this role and within the year or so that I was in it that signaled to me that I was ready for the next step. Others may have considered me too young or that I didn't have enough tenure in the profession, but I knew that I was ready for more. I intended on moving to something greater.

I was able to judge where I was within this role so quickly because of my past experiences and the strength I gained from them. There is a particular joy that comes when you get to a point in your life where you are grounded in who you are, what you've overcome, and where you're going. That vision didn't come by happenstance. I was able to gain clarity and confidence through the tears that I cried, the anger I felt, the disappointments I endured, and the setbacks that were actually set ups. All of these things were, and are, a part of who I am and how I came to be where I am. I am no different from the next person. But I have been able to take in my life's circumstances and turn them into my story, my success.

As I neared the end of the academic school year in the director role, I was actively applying to and interviewing for superintendent positions. I agreed with Dr. Gibson that I was ready for the next step in my career. I knew that if I stayed in this director role, I wouldn't be able to make the strides I wanted because I was bored with the work. It wasn't challenging, and I felt I had stopped developing. I reached the end of one search that I was interested in but wasn't the chosen candidate. Because the academic school year was ending, it would be rare that another position at that level would become available.

I continued on with my director role, yet my thoughts were on how I interviewed and how I could improve in the next opportunity to showcase my expertise. I also reflected on the role itself. I was interviewing for a position that had a retiring superintendent. This person had been in the role for a long time, and there would be large shoes to fill. Additionally, it was rumored that this district might be taken over by the state and monitored closely to meet certain success metrics. I could understand why I wasn't the chosen candidate because this would be my first superintendency, and it was clear that the district needed substantial growth.

Just when I thought I had reflected on how I could be better for the next opportunity and had coped with the disappointment of not getting this role, that same district called me and offered me the position of interim superintendent elect. Apparently, the person they chose as a finalist decided to rescind their acceptance, and they saw me as the "runner up." Because this would be my first role as superintendent, the district wanted me to work alongside the current superintendent for the Fall semester of the academic year. I would be named as the Superintendent in January of the Spring semester.

I could tell when the board offered me the position that the members weren't sure about my abilities. I was clearly a decent enough interviewer, but my lack of district experience made them hesitant. This is why I would, essentially, shadow the current leader in hopes that I would better understand the expectations of the role. I was offered the position around mid to late August with the expectation that I would start in

September. This all happened so fast, and I had just convinced myself that I might have been better off without the position.

I spoke with Dr. Gibson about my hesitations due to the rumors I heard about the district being taken over by the state and how that might reflect on me. This district had issues before my time there, so I wanted to be sure that none of this would impact my future career opportunities. As always, I remembered Mr. Wallace and how he motivated me and challenged me to think about it from a different perspective. He would simply expect me, whether the rumors were true or not, to make the best decision. As I thought, I hadn't run away from any other opportunity in my career before. Why should I start now? This really resonated with me because the thought was right. Why was I doubting myself now? Was I afraid of failure? Of how it might look to the public? To future employers? I prayed about it, consulted my family and close friends and decided to accept the position.

I was nervous about the odd structure of this position as well as stepping into new territory, but I knew that I had done this before. While I had some anxiety, I knew that I could do this again. I also knew that the district had their concerns about my lack of higher-level experience and that I would need to do a bit of proving myself before I could be trusted to take on the role fully. What I was surprised by was the lack of belief from those that I was leading. I could tell that people were used to leading from the classroom and the community. The teachers, staff, and community members were all very vocal and opinionated, and while I appreciated the engagement, I was struck by the opposition I faced. There were many times I felt that people wondered who I thought I was to come into this district and try to change it. I really struggled with this sentiment because in my mind, it was clear that this district was struggling and in jeopardy of being taken over by the state. This is never something that a district wants to happen.

There was a clear distance between the amount of growth needed and the amount of teamwork and buy in those within the district wanted to commit to. At the same time, the structure of the leadership was challenging as well. There were, in essence, two superintendents. It was confusing for those who reported to this position, and it was confusing for me as well. There were some days I felt empowered to make decisions and the superintendent welcomed that. There were other days that it was frowned upon that I would try to move forward on something without their input. This back and forth happened often and there never seemed to be a common approach to anything. It was hard for people to understand who was really in charge. For me, it was not only hard to not have a consistent and strong foundation at work, but it also didn't help me understand the role I was stepping in to. The intent behind allowing for this soft transition was so that I could take on the role intentionally and have the support I needed to succeed.

With the rumors happening in the background, the opinions about my expertise and years of experience, and the odd leadership structure, I was quickly introduced to the political side of my role. Being a superintendent is extremely public and very political. This was always an area that I didn't excel in and found it to be in discord with my value of authenticity. I enjoyed the profession because I was able to focus on the success of children and improving the education system. I understand why and how this can be a political thing for people, but I didn't approach my career that way. I had to balance the expectations of so many constituents while also being mindful of legislation and policies that came from the state and federal levels. This balance can be hard to strike, and the balance shifted often.

By the end of the Fall semester, the superintendent transitioned to retirement, and I was named superintendent that January. This was a mid-year change which created some disruption, but I was excited to lead from *my* perspective, not a shared one. I was now able to set a plan to get to know the school board better and understand their expectations. I also learned quickly to take this experience day by day. No two days were the same, and I had to remain flexible since I didn't know what I might be walking into daily. I had to be strategic about what I took on and finding balance in the work. I had to learn to delegate early within this role. I wasn't able to fully understand and learn my job before I realized I had to delegate some of my tasks to others. This took a great amount of trust, particularly at such a public level.

I was used to rolling up my sleeves and putting in 'elbow grease' to move the needle on success, but this role would expect me to be a public figure in a way that I hadn't before. I had a lot of higher-level interactions with district and state leaders. I had to work through the push and pull of various school needs. Not every school was succeeding, or struggling, in the same way and I had to understand the nuances and then provide the appropriate support and resources to the best of my ability. I had learned how to delegate in my prior roles, but this was different. My team truly had to be to be strong and pull together to achieve, and I had to develop that relationship, even when they may not have trusted me to lead them. There were some things, though, that I just couldn't delegate out and that forced me to be intentional about my time and personal and professional balance.

I oversaw a budget for an entire district of schools, not just one. I knew that money was a quick way to lose your job. Mismanaging funds, not having correct checks and balances, or allocating funds in discord with legislative and policy stipulations could be a major setback in a superintendent's career. I couldn't, and wouldn't, let that happen to me. I kept those high impact items within my purview and worked hard to find some semblance of a personal life as well. I wanted to be more intentional about my time with Erin, and I wanted to be a part of her life in a way that I couldn't for Antonio and Brittany. I wanted to be great in my career, but it couldn't be my everything. This was extremely difficult and a lesson I had many tries to get right. The superintendency gave me the opportunity to embrace all things that came my way and learn from them.

To this day, my first role as a superintendent will always be remembered as bittersweet. Soon after my appointment, the state did indeed take over that district. Because I was new in the role, I didn't take it as a reflection on my abilities, yet I still was disappointed at this decision. I felt I wasn't there long enough to make a difference. There was a Memorandum of Understanding between the district and the state, but the political landscape decided what would become of that district and that was hard to swallow. It was in that moment that the early words of Mr. Wallace started to make sense. He always told me that if I wanted to succeed in this profession, I couldn't be afraid of being fired. At the time I was a young teacher, and it didn't make sense. But seeing how my career could change so quickly and not be based on me or my actions was difficult.

Professional Walk

Most of us are raised to believe that if you work hard and are passionate, you will succeed. Working at the district level let me know that this wasn't always true and there would be many reasons this sentiment couldn't be true. I was so thankful to have had Mr. Wallace in my corner at that time because I was able to pivot my mindset to finishing the year strong, regardless of how it would be transitioning after me. Once the state took over, I wouldn't have a job. Once the announcement was made of this change, the environment shifted to something that could be described as toxic or hostile. People were upset for many reasons, and many were justified. I had my own feelings but being a part of the political landscape now, I couldn't let that show. I had to be that district's superintendent until the end. I had to encourage those I led to continue doing good work because children were at the core of all of this.

As I reflected on this decision, I felt angry. I wondered why the position was even posted. Why didn't they let the previous superintendent retire and then make the transition without bringing in someone new? Why even bring me in and disrupt my life and career? At the same time, because this role was so public, once the decision for the district to move under state leadership was released, the media started to define the narrative, regardless of its accuracy. Family members and friends would call me and ask me what happened and why I was getting fired. Although I could explain the situation to them because we had a personal relationship, I wondered how this might impact my career. If you Googled me, would this show up? How would that impact my reputation? I had nothing to do with this decision; it seemed to be made before me, even *in spite of* me.

It was in this process where I had to truly learn how to reach a place of acceptance. This position didn't allow me to work in ideals; I had to embrace reality. I had to learn how to live with things. I had to adjust my perception of circumstances in a way that would serve me, not keep me stuck in the 'what ifs?' I had to respect the situations I was encountering, regardless of my personal feelings and I learned few hard lessons in this time period. Some may think that I wasn't in the role long enough to learn anything, but it was in the process of this position, and the unique things that occurred, that allowed me exposure to some of the most distinctive experiences possible. As my career seemed to be struggling, I had to remind myself that this was only a part of who I am and the life I lead. It was a great lesson that put a fine point on the fact that your life is not your own unless you keep what is dear to you in a safe place.

If I hadn't been intentional about developing my personal and professional values, I would have found myself in this situation with no compass to guide me. When I felt like a failure and couldn't understand these circumstances, I had to remember that I had been very successful and that this was only one hurdle; this did not stop my future. I also learned in the process what it meant to be so exposed and vulnerable. There are so many things that people are allowed to know about you, or request about the work that you were doing. The media can request emails and budgets, and so much more. Having integrity and being resolute in your decisions are essential to success in a role like this, and this was new territory for me. Without exposure to large scale decisions being made that impact me directly, I wouldn't have known how to approach this situation. I wouldn't have had the exposure to learn how to work with local media and be in partnership with communities to best impact the district.

The last thing I learned from this role was that regardless of the work that you plan to do or the passion that you have, if you don't support some level of the status quo, that will make or break your career. This sentiment ties into the political aspect of the job but more than that, you have to pick your battles. Not every school board member or legislator came to their role and position for the same reasons as you. While I made it a core value to center children and their success in all I did, with every decision that I made, that wasn't necessarily true of those I worked alongside. There are many different perspectives on 'the right thing,' and I learned which of my perspectives were worth fighting for and which would create the least disruptions to my vision.

This was an incredibly hard time in my career as it was the first time I was dealing with disappointment in the public eye. I wanted to be known for the good that I did, the work that I fostered. I didn't want to be held responsible for actions that were out of my control. One very important aspect of this position was the ability to separate out the public opinion and the truth with an understanding that you can only control one of those. Thinking about all of the times I was able to reside on the progress and performance of myself and my team made me realize just how complex leadership in the public education space was. At the time, I had so many frustrations about what was happening, but as I reflect on it now, it was the perfect way to understand how to navigate this role and its dynamics. I was able to see how district level decisions impacted communities, teachers, and students. I was able to view this from a lens of observer since I didn't have anything to do with the decisions being made. I'm now thankful for that opportunity because I was able to move into my next superintendency that much more prepared.

***

Professional Walk

It was in the last month of my first superintendent's role that I learned I wouldn't be returning for another school year. I hadn't prepared to conduct an employment search, nor did I know that I would need to. Given the timing of this announcement, I was left wondering what options I had. Most superintendent positions are filled before the summer even began. I was finishing out a school year, and I had no idea where I was going to be three months later when a new school year would begin. I knew it would be almost impossible to find another lateral role, so I had to consider other district and school level leadership positions. I couldn't afford to be unemployed for the next school year, so I was considering all options.

Throughout my life, I've relied on my own understanding and talents, and that has caused an environment of high expectations and pressure to meet them. I created a space of anxiety over my next steps, and I have been blessed to see the moments when God has stepped in and said, "I've got this." The next step in my career was completely, divinely ordained. I had no idea of what I would do in this transition, and I didn't have many places to look. I was having to consider moving away or looking for lower-level positions so I could find employment. I felt I had a dark mark on my resume due to the district being turned over to the state. Although it had nothing to do with me, I had to be diligent about how I would market myself. How could I explain what happened and have people believe me? I was afraid that my character and integrity would be called into question.

I was battling myself in my mind and trying to convince myself of how to believe what happened, and how I would talk about it. In the midst of this inner turmoil, I saw a position in Jasper County, the county where I had been a principal who rolled up her sleeves and transformed an elementary school with great success. This is where I think God stepped in. I couldn't believe that I was seeing a superintendent position in Jasper County. People knew me there and knew my impact. While I was beating myself up and feeling like a failure, God was orchestrating the perfect transition for me. I thought I had committed professional suicide, and here was God breathing life into my future.

Once I saw this position, I immediately applied. There were other candidates, and it was still competitive. I was feeling I was at a rock bottom time in my life, so I entered those interviews with only my faith and the little bit of fight I had left. I knew what I could do, if only given the chance, so, I had to make them give me a chance. I was living my life through the media headlines and through my personal lens. Those two things didn't align, and I had to remove this from my mind as I interviewed. I believe that because I had been in this district prior to this position opening, there were people there who knew my work and my passion. I didn't have to prove myself as much as I thought I did because I was able to reassert what they already knew about me. I found this process to be a hard lesson in both humiliation and humility. I had to reassess my foundation and confidence and refortify it.

By June, I was appointed as the interim superintendent and was thrilled. While I was happy for a bit more employment security, I was also smarter and had learned from my most recent experience. I spoke with the district lawyer soon after I was appointed and stated my concerns with the interim status. The person in this position before me had only been there for a few years. This made me wonder what level of impact they could have had in that short time. Most superintendents are in the role for at least five years to both transition and then maximize in the role. Having just felt blindsided, I didn't want to be in a position that felt temporary. I didn't want to pour into this district and then be moved around and lose my hard work. I felt conflicted because I was both extremely grateful to have this opportunity, but I also knew my worth. I felt that if I were good enough to interview, I was good enough to be permanent.

I'm so glad that I didn't let the doubts in my mind circumvent the value I knew I brought to this district. Within the next month, I was named as permanent superintendent and went into the school year as such. I knew that I couldn't start this journey grounded in fear; I would fail if so. Given what I had just experienced as well, I resigned myself to the idea that I was essentially working in a contract status. The employment agreement may not have stated that explicitly but similar to what Mr. Wallace told me all those years ago, I had to embody the notion that I was always interviewing for the job and that all eyes were constantly on me.

    I often made time for quiet reflection and time with my journal, and this pivot in my career felt like another one of those times that I needed to center myself. Just a few years before, I was working towards a principalship and that was the goal. Then, I was exposed to the possibility of a superintendency. I had never considered this career path and there I stood. I set out to understand the district level of education so I could strike out on my own and now, I was one of the top leaders in the field. I felt I could see all of the moments aligned before me to make up this journey I had been on. I was moved by all that I had been through to this point. I could feel and remember the bruises and missteps along the way. The things that I thought would break me but instead simply stretched my capacity. I reflected on all of the times where I experienced triumph, times when I persevered, times when I proved to *myself* that I could do this. I was now standing on the precipice of my next chapter of my career when I remembered that years ago, I spoke this into existence. I had stood in the gymnasium of an elementary school in Jasper County years prior, telling those students and teachers that I planned to return as their superintendent. I have, quite literally, no idea why I said that. I wasn't even considering a role at that level- it wasn't on my radar in the slightest. But I said it and I'm confident that God intentionally put it on my mind and heart to say because he knew he would allow it to be true.

***

Living up to my wildest dreams was an exercise of perseverance and adaptability. I stepped into this role with divine confidence and have been met with many obstacles along the way. I have now been the Jasper County Superintendent for five years, and I've led through many successes and failures. I've been clear of mind in my purpose and have also had times of redirection. I've led through a pandemic and watched our society change and thus observe its impact on education. Like many in the field of education and beyond, I have contemplated many aspects of my life and career after having been through so much pain and hardship during the COVID-19 pandemic. I have questioned my work life balance and the values I hold dear. I have sat with myself to discover the things that are most core to my being and been met with worthy examination of those things.

Professional Walk

I think that watching a global generation experience a worldwide health crisis that impacted us all on a cellular level challenged us to think about the paradigms we hold and how we are choosing to live our lives. Many of us in helping professions also re-evaluated the cost of our careers and the role they have played in our lives. The great resignation is an example of the culture shift we are having around the lives we lead and the role of work. Where we once valued accomplishment and 'the hustle,' we now see people who value inner peace and balance in all aspects of their lives. We've also seen changes in our political systems and increased legislation within the field of education from those inside and out of it.

In my career, I have come to regard myself as a change agent. I often consider my tenure within a position to be within a three to five-year timeframe. Some may want the comfort of stability over a longer service time, but I was fortunate to understand my strengths early on. As I consider what is next for the field of education and where I fit in, I am challenged with more now than ever before. How do I lead in a world that feels unfamiliar and so different than it was even three years ago? How do I contribute to the continual success of our students, especially when they're dealing with issues we've not seen before? How do I preserve myself and values in a world that seems unknown to me?

As I ponder these points, I assume that many others are too. Like the many other times in my life where I had to step into uncertainty, I'd like to approach them with the knowledge I've gained thus far. I don't know what may be next for me, but I know that I'll approach it with the grace, curiosity, and confidence I've continually clung to. In this life, I have realized that to make a genuine impact, you have to possess more than tough skin. When my name seemed to be in headline after headline and my foundation seemed to have cracks, I found that remaining steadfast and remembering that I can get through whatever storm I'm in created a sense of peace and allowed for a clear perspective. There were so many points in my life when I allowed fear to make a playground in my mind. Every time I allowed fear to rule my thoughts and actions, I found myself less effective and certainly less content.

Being intentional about removing fear from my leadership was the key to my success. Coupling my high level of integrity and character, with a fearless approach, I was able to lead without personal turmoil. I couldn't be afraid of being fired or making mistakes. I had to embrace that I was, and am, only human. Being a good leader isn't about perfectionism or hiding your weaknesses. It's about embracing all parts of you that also allows others to do the same. I found that endurance and stamina, in addition to old-fashioned grit, made a big impact. Regardless of your career field or aspirations, you will always have champions and challengers. It isn't your job to change their minds or prove your worth. It's your responsibility to not only validate your talents and calling but to also surround yourself with those who will be on this growth journey with you.

I couldn't have led my life, or written this book, without the support of those who have my best interest at heart. These supporters not only care for me but are honest to a fault. I don't encourage surrounding yourself with those who will only revere you without reproach. Refinement, reflection, and the courage to course correct will always serve you along your path. There is a saying that states, "Leadership is lonely." This is true. Not everyone who sets out on your journey with you gets to stay in step with you. It is important, however, to realize that experiencing opposition is not a sign of failure but who you are in the face of it speaks to you as a leader. Success lies in what you do day in and day out, consistently.

There is no set path to leadership or one way to be an extraordinary leader. The amazing thing about being a leader is that your superpower is *you*. You can never underestimate your worth and value. If others don't see that within you, it doesn't mean it doesn't exist. I believe in a higher power and that I was uniquely made with a purpose only I can fulfill. I believe the same of you. Every day, you have the distinct opportunity to go after what you want and earn it. It won't be given to you easily or stumbled upon by accident. Your success is intentional and handcrafted for you. It is up to you to embrace all parts of your journey to get there. There will be times when you make mistakes or veer off of your intended path, but it all leads to the betterment of you. I have many great times in my life, yet the most pivotal times of growth came with great adversity and often pain. I encourage you to embrace the pain just as much as the triumph; it's there to tell you something.

When I challenged myself to get quiet with my fears, doubts, and discomfort, I always found that I was in a place where I didn't want to change. Yet I had to. I had to ask myself questions about my foundation, my core, and where I found myself in proximity to it. Whenever I was able to pinpoint the distance between myself and my purpose, I was able to navigate my compass back to my calling. And, when I found myself going the "wrong way," I gave myself grace and time to make my way back.

As I traverse this next phase of my life after a global tragedy and the ever-changing field of education, I know that whatever life brings, I have the sum of my experiences to embrace it fully. I was a dark-skinned girl from Florence, South Carolina who wanted to change the world. I was a teenage girl who felt she had to fight to prove her worth and defend her success. I was a young Black woman who took a chance on believing in herself. I am now a strong, self-assured professional who has no plans of disappointing the versions of myself that have come before me. It is every iteration of myself that has led to the life I currently lead, and it is all of those versions of me that I will carry with me the rest of the way.

Acknowledgments

To my Heavenly Father…Glory, Halleluiah! Thank you, Most High, for your continued Grace and Mercy!

To My Loving Father and Mother, Richard and Mozella. The foundation you built for me is so strong! I appreciate the sacrifices made on my behalf.

To My Children, Antonio, Brittany, and Erin! I appreciate your understanding of my time devoted to reading and helping others. It was all to pave the way for the three of you.

To My Brother Richard! Thank you for always being there for me and for ensuring that I understood my worth!

To My Late Grandmother, Mozella! I will never forget my morals and values. I have truly learned how to "Build a Bridge and get over it!"

To My Mentor Calvin Wallace! You instilled in me the value of never being afraid to be fired from any job. Instead, you taught me to always remain sharp regarding my skillset so that I can stand on my own two feet.

To Sabrina! Thank you for encouraging me to express my professional path in print.

To My Prayer Warriors! Thank you for praying and continuing to pray!

Professional Walk

www.ingramcontent.com/pod-product-compliance
Lightning Source LLC
Chambersburg PA
CBHW041129110526
44592CB00020B/2736